Rage and Resistance

Studies in Women and Religion /
Études sur les femmes et la religion

Studies in Women and Religion is a series designed to serve the needs of established scholars in this new area, whose scholarship may not conform to the parameters of more traditional series with respect to content, perspective, and/or methodology. The series will also endeavour to promote scholarship on women and religion by assisting new scholars in developing publishable manuscripts. Studies published in this series will reflect the wide range of disciplines in which the subject of women and religion is currently being studied, as well as the diversity of theoretical and methodological approaches that characterize contemporary women's studies. Books in English are published by Wilfrid Laurier University Press.

Inquiries should be directed to the series coordinator Eleanor J. Stebner (Faculty of Theology, University of Winnipeg, Winnipeg).

Studies in Women and Religion /
Études sur les femmes et la religion
Volume 11

Rage and Resistance

A Theological Reflection on the Montreal Massacre

Theresa O'Donovan

Published for the Canadian Corporation for Studies in Religion/
Corporation Canadienne des Sciences Religieuses
by Wilfrid Laurier University Press

2007

This book has been published with the help of a grant from the Canadian Federation for the Humanities and Social Sciences, through the Aid to Scholarly Publications Programme, using funds provided by the Social Sciences and Humanities Research Council of Canada. We acknowledge the financial support of the Government of Canada through the Book Publishing Industry Development Program for our publishing activities.

Library and Archives Canada Cataloguing in Publication

O'Donovan, Theresa M., 1956–
    Rage and resistance : a theological reflection on the Montreal massacre / Theresa O'Donovan.

(Studies in women and religion ; 11)
Includes bibliographical references and index.
ISBN-10: 0-88920-522-1
ISBN-13: 978-0-88920-522-2

    1. Montréal École Polytechnique Women Students Massacre, Montréal, Quebec, 1989. 2. Women—Crimes against—Religious aspects—Christianity. 3. Women—Violence against. 4. Church and social problems. I. Title. II. Series.

HV6535.C33M65 2006   261.8'331523082   C2006-906203-X

Contents

Preface

This is a travelogue. It charts the course of my journey into a foreign country. Strangely enough, that foreign country is the one I know most intimately, the one that I call home: Canada. Why foreign, then? Because in 1989, in December, the country I thought I knew changed. I realize now that it was not so much that Canada changed but that I did, as I began to see this country differently, newly, as through the eyes of a stranger.

On December 6, 1989, a twenty-five-year-old man armed with a semi-automatic weapon entered an engineering school in Montreal and, over the course of approximately twenty minutes, shot fourteen women dead before killing himself. I wonder what it must be like to hear that for the first time.

> *"Women? I thought engineering was primarily a male pursuit?"*
> "It is."
> *"Then how did it happen that only women were killed?"*
> "It didn't just happen. The women were separated out, targeted, and murdered."
> *"But why?"*

Yes, why? That was certainly the question in the immediate aftermath of the murders, and it is still debated today, more than a decade and a half later. "Why" is perhaps the question that most accurately encapsulates what it is to be human. It is indicative of our desire—our desperate need—to make sense of the world around us. This is one story of an attempt to make sense of what happened on that day in December and in the years following. It intersects with the stories of many others—people I have met only on the printed page, and artists, musicians, academics, and activists across Canada who met with me during the summer of 2003 to share their own understandings of and responses to the Montreal Massacre.

As are many stories, mine is convoluted. It begins in Africa. From 1978 to 1980, with a newly minted BA in hand, I taught on a small island off the coast of Sierra Leone under the auspices of Volunteer International Christian Service. It was there I first learned that the world was not what I thought it to be. Feminist theologian Beverly Wildung Harrison writes that "for each of us, critical consciousness is forged ... by acknowledging the social contradictions that shape not only our collective existence but our personal lives as well. Awareness of contradiction ... comes from a process of concrete engagement."[1] Immersion in countless contradictions in Sierra Leone prompted my initial forays toward a critical consciousness, a consciousness that became well established when I taught in a small Christian community in a remote corner of Nicaragua from 1984 to 1986. There, too, contradiction was the stuff of life. There was no correlation between what I read in the Sandinista paper *La Barricada* and heard on the United States–based Voice of America, little agreement between the popular church and the hierarchical church, few similarities between the life I was living and the one I remembered. The gaps were not neutral; the definitions articulated by those with power were armed. Ronald Reagan's interpretation of the Nicaraguan "threat" meant death for many. My decision to study theology developed from a desire to put into theological perspective the reality I encountered in Nicaragua, a reality that contained both death and destruction but also exuberant hope, every reason to despair and as many reasons not to. Over the years I also became concerned for Canadian reality, realizing contradiction is the stuff of life for many in this country as well.

In Canada, too, definitions are armed. On December 6, 1989, a gunman's interpretation of a feminist "threat" meant death for fourteen women. My initial attempt to make some sense of that event took the form of a doctoral thesis analyzing the presentation of, responses to, and debates over the massacre in the weeks and year that followed, and the theological implications of that analysis. Writing the last few paragraphs of the dissertation should have provided some kind of closure, but it did not. There was no personal resolution because there had been no communal one. Today, violence directed towards women continues unabated.

So the analyzing and writing continues as well. This time through I have considered more extensively responses to the murders that were not primarily word oriented, in art and music for example, viewing them as manifestations of a spirituality of resistance. A grant from the Wabash Centre for Teaching in Theology and Religion allowed me to visit Halifax, London, Montreal, Ottawa, Toronto, Vancouver, and Waterloo to interview a variety of people who responded to December 6th. Their commitment to the forging of a changed world is as much a part of the Canadian landscape as the gunman who raged against that possibility. My sincere thanks to Beth Alber, Rita Beiks, Susan Boyd, Elaine Carol, Dorothy Chunn, Regina Coupar, Kim Dawn, Peter Davison, Monique Frize, Chris McDowell, Martin Dufresne, Rose-Marie Goulet, Pamela Harrison, Maggie Helwig, Suzanne Jay, Michele Landsberg, Lynn Moore, Brigitte Neumann, Bernice Vincent, Carol Ann Weaver, and Hildegard Westerkamp.

Introduction: Roughing It in the Bush

Feminist theology, like all liberation theologies, arises from the concrete struggle of particular people with a particular historical context.... The "painstaking hermeneutic" of actual Canadian conditions has to be our starting point.　　　　　　— Ruth Evans, *A Long and Faithful March*

Look out your window. The world you see laid out before you is so very different from the one that greeted our immigrant ancestors. Generations ago, Susanna Moodie looked out her window onto a harsh and lonely wilderness. The woman who had left England in 1832 for the backwoods of Upper Canada shared the plight of many immigrants, her hopes quickly dimmed in the face of illness, poverty, and a land that seemingly defied comprehension. Moodie "entered a large darkness" when she left behind her civilized distinctions to make a home in the Canadian wilderness, according to Margaret Atwood's poetic revisioning of Moodie's reflections. She gazed on "vistas of desolation" and heard "malice in the trees' whispers."[1] She faced terror. She buried her children.

Mrs. Moodie, "who once viewed it with hatred so intense that [she] longed to die," came eventually to love Canada.[2] The wilderness changed her. The wilderness itself changed. "The country is the same only in name," she wrote, several years after her arrival. "The rough has become smooth, the crooked has been made straight, the forests have been converted into fruitful fields."[3]

We have come far, and now look out upon a country rich and prosperous. But wait, there is still something lurking in the shadows. Something

1

grim and dangerous. The wilderness *has* changed, but Canada is still a large darkness for many of its women. The contemporary Canadian wilderness is not geographically contained; it "is not a place, but a category, defined as much by absences and contrasts as by positives and characteristics."[4] For women, it is defined by an everyday and often unquestioned violence and both subtle and unsubtle diminishment. It is sketched out endlessly in the pages of local newspapers. Page after page, day after day, one reads of attacks, abuse, and blame: funding cuts to women's groups; misogyny at the movies; bodies in fields. And page after page, day after day, the accounts are as neatly confined and defined as the columns on the page. The fact of violence and the lack of connection to other facts of violence are standard daily fare. The wilderness is deep. The measure of the darkness was made known at an engineering school one early winter evening in 1989. On December 6, a gunman entered the University of Montreal's Ecole Polytechnique. Blaming feminists for ruining his life, he murdered fourteen women before killing himself. What would you write now, Mrs. Moodie, about this land?

The story I want to write is this. Fourteen women were murdered on December 6, 1989, by a man who claimed he hated feminists. They were mostly engineering students finishing the term, no doubt looking forward to the holidays. "Safely through another one," I can imagine them thinking. Perhaps some of them felt uncomfortable, from time to time, being in a primarily male environment, but unsafe? Who knows? He entered a classroom, separated the men from the women, and shot as many women as he could. In the end, fourteen women dead, nine more injured, and four injured men. Fourteen women hunted down and killed. The murder of those women that awful day claimed me. Those who were killed were not "my people" in the personal, intimate sense: they were not my sisters, my friends, my classmates. But nonetheless, December 6, 1989, impacted me personally and intimately. As a woman at a university, I identified with the women murdered. Even more profoundly, that day changed the way I see. It was a moment of disclosure, of illumination. Not "a soft light dawning" illumination, but that of an exploding bomb: a sudden flash that reveals the carnage, the silhouette of broken buildings scorched into the sky. It was no longer possible to believe that "it's not really *that* bad." The ugly face of hate and violence was laid bare.

Shock and mourning were the immediate reactions, accompanied by efforts to make sense of what had happened. "Making sense" took the form of variant, often volatile readings which led more than once to heated exchanges. "An isolated incident, the incomprehensible act of a madman," some insisted. Others saw it as the extreme end of an all-too-common continuum of violence against women. There were those who positioned the massacre within the context of family violence: the murderer was himself the victim of abuse, and his own history exploded into the horror of December 6. Still others described the murders as the inevitable consequence of feminist social destabilization. These are not simply differences of opinion that should be quietly heard and respected—you're entitled to your view and I'm entitled to mine—they are distinct, conflictual understandings of the world that have real consequences for how we organize and work in the society in which we live.

The murders prompted much more than a struggle over meaning, of course, and the responses were many and varied. The police, media, coroner, and government spokespeople sprang into action and responded as was appropriate to each particular domain: as a matter of public security, as a significant news event, as a matter for investigation, in the interests of public relations. "The scale, reportability, and associated characteristics of the massacre make of it a tragic public event, indeed, a *public disaster.* As such it comes under the purview of public officials, that is, the political leaders—the mayor, the provincial premier, the relevant cabinet minister, the prime minister."[5] Public officials and members of the mainstream media were not the only ones who were galvanized. People took to the streets, to churches, to auditoriums, to art galleries, to the halls of power. Conferences were organized, art exhibits staged, funds raised, politicians lobbied. Poetry, plays, and songs were composed, videos filmed, and permanent memorials erected. Yearly, from coast to coast, commemorative events of every kind mark the anniversary. These responses to the murders revealed something of the resiliency of the human spirit in the face of seemingly unbearable anguish; they revealed something of our dauntless capacity to resist.

These numerous and collective efforts have had an effect. It is now possible to point with some satisfaction to a series of accomplishments, including more widespread awareness of the issue of violence against women. In the early days and months, the view that the massacre was an isolated act of insanity held sway. Three weeks after the massacre, a poll indicated that 60 per cent of Canadians saw it as not connected to the wider context of violence against women.[6] That interpretation has now been largely displaced, and the massacre is widely understood as part of a continuum of violence that must be acknowledged and eradicated; in 1991, December 6 was declared a national day of remembrance and action on violence against women. There have been government hearings on the issue, reforms to gun control legislation, an increase in the number of women enrolled in faculties of engineering, and numerous other initiatives.

Can we finally relax? Can we leave behind what some people see as a morbid preoccupation with the Montreal Massacre? Can we let the women rest in peace, as one *Globe and Mail* columnist entreated the day after its tenth anniversary? No. While it *is* true that there is an increased awareness of the range and extent of violence against women and a greater capacity to see individual acts of violence within a broader context, the violence continues. Countless words have been shed over the Montreal Massacre, like blood spilling forth from a wound, unstaunchable. And still there is more to say.

That is the narrative line I will expand and interrogate in the pages that follow. I refer to my presentation as narrative quite deliberately. We have no definitive access to "what really happened" at Ecole Polytechnique on December 6; we have only what we make of it. Pauline Greenhill's representation of the massacre as a cultural text is to the point:

> Most of what took place the afternoon and evening of the event can never be known or understood. Contrary to the belief of those who feel that the search for facts and the truth need be in vain, any account of something that happened, whether written, told, photographed or video-taped, cannot avoid being interpretive. It is affected, even while data is being collected, by the limitations of the medium chosen—what it can and cannot frame. Action in time and space is thus translated into some kind of visual and/or semiotic system.
>
> The production of any account is also influenced by the perceptions and individual personalities of its creators, by the passage of time and by perspective.... Ultimately ... we select the significant from the insignificant according to subjective principles which include theories and methods.... Reality cannot be recovered. There are only the interpretations— our attempts to give events meaning and make them, at the very least, comprehensible."[7]

My attempt to give events meaning and make them comprehensible focuses on examining how the massacre was "taken up" by the media, experts, politicians, and countless individuals and groups, and with what results. What is revealed about the Canadian landscape? The murders and responses to them say much about what it is to be a woman in Canada. That women were the targets, that the struggle over whose knowledge would define it was so hotly engaged, that the violence continues—these facts are revelatory. As such, an examination of responses to the massacre is an examination of significant features of the Canadian social, political, and cultural terrain. It is an examination of the structures, processes, and understandings that constrain us, and of the ways we protest and resist.

This narrative joins and relies upon many other analyses and commentaries on December 6, among them *The Montreal Massacre,* a collection of letters and essays written by Quebec feminists addressing the murders and the world in which they happened (1991); the National Film Board documentary *After the Montreal Massacre* (1990); Maureen Bradley's documentary *Reframing the Montreal Massacre* (1995), which considers how the media shaped understandings of the murders; and Peter Eglin and Stephen Hester's *The Montreal Massacre: A Story of Membership Categorization Analysis* (2003). What is unique to my presentation is that I consider the murders and the myriad responses to them from a theological perspective. One of the tasks of theology is to articulate and clarify the struggles in which we are engaged—to *name* our reality, both the forces that oppress and the possibilities for resistance and healing. A grasp of the specific forms and processes of our oppression can help clarify what is necessary for social change.[8] But clarification alone is insufficient. In order to act, we require both material and spiritual resources. An appreciation of efforts to challenge destructive actions and structures can focus our collective energies to resist that which hurts, harms, diminishes, and kills us.

I want to reply to the friend who asks, But why theology at all? For both of us, many of the traditional theological categories have lost their power to inspire. Yet each of us has cast her lot with those who struggle; we are compelled by a thirst for justice, made tenacious by hope, and cannot but continue to affirm life in the midst of systematic denials of life.[9] If we let go of theology because it has so often proven oppressive to women, we also let go of its creative potential; at its best, theology has the power to compel, to grasp the heart and imagination, to appeal to those for whom the language of liberation is mother tongue. But even if we let go, there is no letting go. As Elisabeth Schüssler Fiorenza writes, "Western women are not able to discard completely and forget our personal, cultural, or religious Christian history. We will either transform it into a new liberating future or continue to be subject to its tyranny whether we recognize its power or not."[10]

This analysis follows a distinctive theological path, that of a practical, contextual theology. Contextual theology does not look heavenward, searching for universal answers to abstract questions. Rather, it requires that we look unflinchingly at the world in which we live, using analytic tools that best uncover the structures, processes, and modes of thinking that constrain both life and spirit. The intent is ultimately practical—to transform structures and processes that are life denying. A practical contextual theology is both analytic and strategic, with an intent not only to describe the world but to change it. In adopting such an approach I stand with those contextual/liberation/feminist theologians who "presume that analysis of historical contradiction is *the* starting point of the theological process itself."[11] "Liberation theologians ... do not try to discover and describe universal conditions for the possibility of sin; they try to unmask the myriad manifestations of particular forms of sin, particular forms of domination.... The task of liberation theology is to break the facade of innocence and expose the impact of our social system."[12]

A focus on a particular context does not leave us stranded in the immediate and local. The particular, shaped by the broader political–cultural landscape, is a point of entry into larger social and economic processes.[13] What is happening to us here and now "is part of what's happening to other women—other people—elsewhere in the world. And here and now ... is the only place to begin. This is the only way we can begin to know how to act ... to organize ... to struggle."[14]

This path cannot be walked alone. As a Canadian woman writing for and within a theological community, whose commitment is to women, whose desire is to "grasp the specific forms and processes of [our] oppression—so that we can see what it is, how it is there, and perhaps be clearer about how to work for change"[15]—I turn to two authors who provide resources for grappling with the particular contours of Canada. Both Gregory Baum and Dorothy Smith have written about the need to address the Canadian context; each outlines an approach to it. Baum, an influential and self-consciously Canadian theologian, provides guidelines for thinking which not only allow but demand that the social reality in which we live and move and have our beings—and meet our deaths—be addressed.

"Faith makes people critics of the present order,"[16] Baum tells us; theology itself calls for critical social analysis in order that social evil might be understood and conversion from ideological distortion possible.[17] I follow his lead; the compass he provides is an articulation of the theological imperative to address the context in which our lives are embedded, as well as criteria for best realizing that end. Conditions of possibility for realizing this imperative can be found in the work of sociologist Dorothy Smith. Her project of creating a sociology for women has evolved from a desire for a systematic knowledge of society developed from the standpoint of women. Her method of inquiry starts from the position of individuals in the everyday world and is directed at illuminating how their world is shaped by social processes that go beyond it. Its purpose is to expand our grasp of our experience and the power of our speech by disclosing the relations that organize our oppression—to reveal how it happens as it does.[18] I also engage the work of many women and men who have commented on, analyzed, and responded to the murders at Ecole Polytechnique in the many years following. I approach the work of Baum, Smith, et al. in the same manner that Smith approaches Marx, seizing "upon what [they] offer us as a means of exploring the dynamic of relations in which our lives are caught up."[19] Although I intend to be faithful to their work, the strategy I adopt here is less concerned with its exhaustive representation than with the gathering up of resources in order to apply them to a determined end. This reflects my fundamental conviction about the purpose of scholarship: to empower. Academic work is useful insofar as it reflects—and reflects on—the material and social conditions of peoples' lives in a way that encourages change and helps to create the conditions that make change possible. I engage the work of Baum, Smith, and many others, not for the sake of the engagement but rather for the sake of movement toward a point from which it is possible to sketch significant features of the socially constituted contours of the Canadian landscape. My purpose is not merely descriptive, however; it is to incite action, to compel ever greater resistance to violence and injustice.

As a nation, we have embarked on a collective journey over these years, trying to make sense of the Montreal Massacre, to make changes in the way our society understands and structures itself, and to create memorials to ensure we do not forget the lives taken on December 6, 1989, and on every other day. In these pages I embark on a parallel journey, walking beside that path and reflecting on it from a theological perspective. The massacre and responses to it provide an opening, a window into patterns of exercising power in this society and an incitement to do "the critical task of the believing community:" theology.[20] One of the traditional definitions of theology is "faith seeking understanding." Perhaps it can be defined also as "understanding seeking faith." I *understand,* in my bones and flesh, the violence to which women are sometimes subject. I seek "faith": the courage to name sin and evil, a reason to hope, a community in solidarity, and a language that empowers us to work for justice, for change.

1: Mapping a Way Through

Whether the wilderness is
real or not
depends on who lives there.

— Margaret Atwood, *The Journals of Susanna Moodie*

Susanna Moodie looked out onto an often hostile landscape. Her survival depended in part on learning to understand the land and sky. What did the blackening clouds foretell? What lay hidden beneath the feet and feet of snow? "The problem of the explorer or the settler is an epistemological one, a puzzling out of the ways by which we can know the reality that surrounds us."[1] This too is my problem, one I share with many Canadian women who find the place we inhabit inhospitable. The massacre in Montreal is darkness descended on a forced march through the wilds. How might we come to know the reality around us? How might we map a way through the wilderness? And at what cost? As Atwood's Moodie allowed the land to break in upon her, she began to see beyond the delusions of those who refused the reality that surrounded them, a refusal that sustained some and drove others mad.[2] For her, "the truth [was] necessary, and her ability to perceive the darker side of knowledge—'the dark/ side of light'—[was] an essential part of her quest for survival in the new world, even if such dark knowledge … thrust her into a disordered nightmare."[3] It is December 6, a day that has come to signify death for me, that is my nightmare. Rosemary Radford Ruether writes that "unless one is willing to take the journey into that deeper anger, even to risk going a bit mad, one really will never understand the depths of the evil of sexism."[4] The journey begins.

Gregory Baum

I turn to Canadian theologian and social critic Gregory Baum as guide, a man who has a long history of grappling with "the social imperative," the theological imperative to engage the world in which we live. "The task of practical theology in any country includes at the very beginning a critical analysis of society's structured injustices,"[5] writes Baum. A context of violence does not fill Baum's horizon as it does mine, but he does articulate the theological imperative to begin where we are. He provides the wherewithal to say that *this* world, a world dangerous for women, is theologically significant, that liberation is possible only if we name the plague under which people suffer,[6] and that looking upon the world from its underside reveals its dark ambiguity: "Only if we look at society in solidarity with the oppressed do we recognize its true character."[7]

The appeal to Baum jars, perhaps. He has relatively little to say about women, while bishops and popes loom large. Although he writes often and well about the necessity of dialogue between theology and critical sociology, he appears to be unfamiliar with one of its most creative and critical manifestations: feminist sociology. What he does offer is a long history of grappling with the theological mandate to address the world around us. Even more importantly, perhaps, he offers a challenge: to an "unreserved faith-commitment to social justice and social struggle."[8] Engagement is more than an intellectual exercise.

Who is this man? Born in Berlin in 1923 into a secular Jewish family, Baum left Germany at sixteen just before World War II. He joined the Augustinian Order in 1947 and trained in Thomistic theology at the University of Fribourg, Switzerland, where he received his doctorate in 1956. At the time he believed he was acquiring an approach that would serve him throughout his theological career, but the ecclesiastical renewal of Vatican II demanded modifications to his ideas. Under the pressure of new experiences, he and other theologians of his generation "set out to find new approaches to theological reflection, and [have] kept on moving ever since."[9] While this does not adequately describe all theologians of his generation, it is certainly true that Gregory Baum has "kept on moving." He has moved in and out of favour: asked to help prepare documents for the

Second Vatican Council, he later resigned from the priesthood in 1976 after differences with his order. He has moved around the world, both physically and in solidarity, particularly with those who suffer under unjust structures. He moves readily into conversation, the breadth of his interest and the sheer number of his dialogue partners apparent in even a cursory perusal of the titles of his many articles and books. He has moved into national prominence: in 1990 Baum was named an Officer of the Order of Canada.

His theology, too, has moved. Baum began his theological career as an ecumenist, convinced of the need for Catholic–Protestant and Christian–Jewish dialogue. The movement introduced him to dialogue as a way of truth and as a theological method, a method that gives theological thinking a certain provisional character, always open to new perspectives. During the 1960s, the influence of Karl Rahner's theology and Vatican II's new openness to the world led to a second phase of Baum's theology. He began to look upon theology as humanist in orientation and relied "greatly on psychotherapeutic insights into the transformation of personal life."[10] A third shift in his theological orientation was inspired by his study of sociology at the New School of Social Research in New York from 1969 to 1971. Baum believed that sociology could help him understand why the Catholic church had been unable to embrace the theology outlined in the documents of Vatican II.[11] But the encounter with critical social theory did more than answer nagging questions; it profoundly influenced his entire theological thinking. Since that time Baum's theological research and reflection have focused on the social dimension of the Gospel and on vital social issues, including the role of the church in them.[12] "Without giving up [his] ecumenical and humanistic concerns, [Baum] turned to the more radical critique of church and society, generated by the preferential option for the powerless. [He] came to identify [himself] with what after Johann Baptist Metz is called 'political theology.'"[13]

My engagement with Baum's theology is limited to his third phase, the inception of which corresponds to his decision to study sociology "in the hope of finding principles and methods useful for theology."[14] I focus primarily on his work as it establishes the need for contextual theologies and sociology as theological partner. His work is also used to establish the Montreal Massacre, its aftermath, and embeddedness as an appropriate object of theological inquiry, and Dorothy Smith as an appropriate dialogue partner.

Theology and Sociology

Popular wisdom about the distinction between theology and the social sciences says that the social sciences have to do with the way the world *is*; theology questions the meaning and value of life. Sociology explains events; theology declares their significance.[15] "A sociology is a systematically developed consciousness of society and social relations."[16] Theology is "faith seeking understanding." Even though the two disciplines share common ground in addressing interpersonal and social relations, the explanatory models and categories of each are commonly considered to be fundamentally different, if not antagonistic. Baum's writings over the last four decades significantly challenge these popular distinctions, showing that the presumed divisions between theology and sociology, between the transcendent and the worldly, are simplistic. Baum articulates the implications, for both theology and Christian practice, of starting with a systematic analysis of structured injustice; he establishes criteria for choosing among the various sociological paradigms and makes use of sociological concepts and insights to understand and explain conflicts and changes in the church. He assesses theology using categories derived from the social sciences, develops and defines theological categories using sociological resources, and reads sociology theologically. In short, "Baum shows how social sciences are essential for establishing the very meaning of theological conceptions as well as their necessary political consequences.... Social analysis enters intrinsically into the very method of theology."[17]

To establish the appropriateness of the Montreal Massacre as subject of inquiry and Dorothy Smith as dialogue partner, I consider below Baum's "Three Theses on Contextual Theology," which outline *why* theology must address its context (for theological reasons), *how* that context can best be addressed (in dialogue with a critical, emancipatory sociology), and *from what vantage point* (from the perspective of those who suffer). This essay, supplemented by his other writings of relevant interest, is both a well-developed and representative illustration of Baum's fundamental understanding of the relationship between theology and sociology. It includes several of the recurring themes of his work, and is particularly well suited to the task at hand. I seize upon what he offers us.

Gregory Baum's "Three Theses on Contextual Theology"

Thesis 1: "Theology must analyze and critically reflect upon its historical context for reasons that are properly theological."[18]

Traditional philosophers and theologians believed that ideas were universal, that they transcended their historical context. But dialogue with the sociology of knowledge, Enlightenment criticism, and a variety of the Church's pastoral experiences have shown that "ideas, symbols, moral imperatives, and theological concepts do not float above history; they are grounded in certain historical situations, they are uttered by people who wrestle with the concrete conditions of their existence."[19] In turn, ideas, articulated in a particular social context, have social impact. They may reinforce the dominant culture or the forces that react against it. Theologians need to be cognizant of the political implications of their formulations and evaluate them in terms of Gospel values.

To illustrate this point, Baum looks at understandings of sin. Understanding sin as being solely personal has questionable political consequences insofar as it excuses political and economic institutions from examination. Sin is both personal and social; naming sin must include the socio-political order. "Theologians who clarify the meaning of sin and redemption today must attend to the historical context in which the Church and the theological community find themselves."[20] It is not sufficient simply to recognize sin if that implies condemnation without analysis. Elsewhere Baum writes that he is an advocate of "hard" liberation, which identifies and names the plague that makes people suffer, analyzes the structural causes of oppression, and projects a more just society in discontinuity with the present one.[21] "Hard" liberation differs from "soft" liberation, which speaks of love and justice in general and offends no one. The terms are unfortunate, given the cultural association of these words with masculine and feminine attributes, but the differentiation between the two approaches is significant. All too often, generalized exhortations to love and forgiveness have served to reinforce unjust relations rather than challenge them. Traditional theology trivializes human suffering in history by focusing on the universal rather than the particular, leaving the concrete reality of oppression and destruction unchallenged.[22]

While concern for context is a historical development, "the imperative calling theologians to critical reflection is derived from theology itself."[23] In the Scriptures, faith is presented as an encounter with God's word as judgment (implying the recognition of sin and a turning toward God) and as new life (a new perception of reality and openness to the future).[24] Faith is a praxis, a truth-seeking impulse that critically engages the political order with a view to transforming unjust social structures. An encounter with God's word "includes the recognition of sin in its personal and social dimension, repentance, and the raising of consciousness in regard to the destructive trends operative in one's world."[25]

I return to the Montreal Massacre, asking, with Dorothy Smith, "How is the world in which we act and suffer put together?"[26] This question, and the appeal to a sociology that might disclose the lineaments of a world daily confronted and confronting, does not represent the abandonment of theology, its surrender to social science, or theology's estrangement from its own substance and inspiration. It is no longer possible to theologize in abstract and universal terms as if people's concrete, historical experiences did not count.[27] Fidelity to the divine word demands a listening to present experience[28]—to the anguish and anger precipitated by the act of a man on a murderous hunt for women. But "people's experience by itself is not enough. It is necessary to make sense of this experience, to analyze the historical causes of oppression, and to relate this experience to other forms of domination."[29] "The causes of suffering can be analyzed; there is nothing mysterious about them."[30] And they must be analyzed. Genuine liberation is possible only if the structural sins of society are recognized and named. Theologies which speak of injustice and social change without analyzing the concrete forms of social oppression do not help us to act and make strategies in an evil world.[31] Analysis is necessary in order to perceive the requirements of justice.[32] There must be dialogue between theology and the social sciences in order that social evil might be understood (the ever-present evil that erupted horrifically in Montreal), and conversion from ideological distortion possible (distortions such as those that render violence titillating).[33] Analysis of social context is a theological imperative. Its corresponding mandate is to work toward realizing the requirements of justice—praxis. Paulo Freire's classic understanding of praxis as our action and reflection upon our world in order to transform it is eminently applicable here.[34]

Thesis 11: "Theology affects the choice of the sociological approach for analyzing the social context."

In order to better understand the social context to which they belong, theologians turn to sociological studies.[35] Given that sociology is a diverse field, choices must be made from among a variety of approaches based upon both scientific and theological considerations. In "Humanistic sociology" Baum elaborates on these two hermeneutics. From a scientific perspective, "it must be shown that the interpretation makes sense, that it takes into account the available data, that it sheds light on connected phenomena, and that it explains relations that were hitherto obscure."[36] It should uncover the structures and attitudes of domination and bring to consciousness the subjectivity of the researcher.[37] "But the choice of a paradigm is not purely an exercise in scientific rationality. The option also includes a philosophical dimension. All sociological theory has implicit in it a philosophy of human life."[38] Sociological research always operates out of a value perspective. Baum favours "a sociology that aims at justice, fosters emancipation and promotes humanity."[39]

In "Three Theses" Baum discusses theories that present a sociology of evil applicable to the contemporary world. The first identifies social instability, the undermining of personal and social identities, as the principle cause of social evil. Strengthening order in society is the requisite counter. Baum is critical of this analysis because it ignores social justice, eschews cultural critique, and fosters a conservative law and order mentality that focuses on stability and security. The second theory Baum presents "locates the dehumanizing trends in modern society in the growing power of technology and bureaucracy."[40] Many people in society feel impotent in the face of the mega-structures of modernity—big government, big corporations, and global economic systems. Baum considers this analysis also inadequate because it trivializes issues of political and economic oppression. Theories of alienation based on the impact of technocracy "relativize the plight of the poor, the hungry, the marginal, the exploited."[41] The theory Baum finds most adequate is found in "conflict sociology" which identifies sources of dehumanization in structures of oppression and domination built into economic systems. The theme of oppression resonates with the biblical exodus story, the prophets' demand for social justice, and Jesus's challenge of the powers that destroy life. The official teachings of some Christian churches have followed a form of conflict sociology by recognizing injustice and marginalization as principal sources of evil in society. Since society is a conflictual reality, Christians should understand it through an identification with the oppressed and marginalized, adopting a "preferential option for the poor."[42]

Baum has written often of the significance of this hermeneutic turn. "The public acknowledgement of the preferential option for the poor represents a turning point in the life of the Church that may well turn out to be of world-historical importance…. In the important ecclesiastical documents, the preferential option is presented as a radical response of faith to divine revelation and an expression of discipleship with disturbing, society-shaking consequences."[43] Preferential solidarity includes a double commitment, hermeneutic and activist, a commitment "to look at the social reality from the perspective of the poor … [and] to give public witness to solidarity with these poor."[44] It implies a socio-critical perspective guiding both the perception of society and an active engagement to transform it.[45] The hermeneutic dimension involves listening to victims and turning to appropriate categories to diagnose the historical factors that cause oppressive conditions.[46] It has epistemological implications. One's world description is contingent upon one's place within the world, and some descriptions are more reliable than others. Society can be correctly understood only if we study it from the perspectives of its victims.[47]

The murders in Montreal sparked heated debates over whether the massacre was "an extreme expression of a violence-prone male hostility towards women that [is] tragically commonplace"[48] or an isolated, individual, and tragic act of a lone madman. Behind each of these perspectives is a social theory, whether articulated or not. The theologian intent on investigating the event must consciously and deliberately adopt a perspective from which to engage it, based on rational/scientific and theological considerations. Choices must be made, "for the theologian must decide whether to join the dominant discourse or … turn to a counter discourse"[49]—to join those who see the massacre as a tragic, isolated act, or those who view the act and see the world.

Thesis III: "In the Canadian context theology must be based on preferential solidarity."[50]

It is readily apparent to many people that conflict sociology and an "option for the poor" apply to Third World countries where a small elite dominates the vast majority of people who live in poverty, but "even in this developed country, social justice demands that people choose between solidarity with society's victims or the defense of the existing order."[51] Baum maintains that multiple patterns of domination in Canada, which appear unrelated—the oppression of indigenous people, economic dependency on the United States, regional disparities, racism, and women's subordination, for example—"are in fact built around the present economic system." To make his point, Baum refers to several Canadian Catholic pastoral documents that link oppressive conditions in Canadian society to the economic system, a system held in place by political institutions and the cultural mainstream.[52] "The cultural symbols of Canadians, mediated by various cultural institutions, including the mass media, the schools, and the impact of the market economy, disguise the structures of oppression; they make invisible society's victims and legitimate the inherited economic order."[53] In this context, "theology must introduce an element of rupture in regard to the dominant culture. It must be based on solidarity with the victims."[54]

Although I fully endorse Baum's proposition that theology in Canada must be based on preferential solidarity, I do not subscribe to the subsuming of multiple forms of oppression under an economic rubric. In *Religion and Alienation*, an earlier work, Baum writes that it is unrealistic "to look for a single form of oppression in North America, to which all others are subordinated. What we have is a complex intermeshing of technocratic depersonalization and immobility, economic domination and exploitation, racial exclusion and inferiorization, and other forms including the subjugation of women."[55] The multiple forms of oppression and marginalization in North America are certainly interconnected, but not reducible to one overarching factor. Misogyny cannot be understood or explained through an economic lens alone. Nor do I adhere to Baum's theological program as he describes it in Thesis III: "As in Latin America, theology in a Canadian context must demonstrate from the Scriptures that God is on the side of the poor and judges mainstream culture; second, theology must engage in a systematic critique of the inherited spirituality and theology; third, it must present the Christian message in such a way that people are drawn toward solidarity *of* the poor and *with* the poor, and move toward seeing society as a social project for which they are responsible."[56] My own starting point is not scripture, not even theology per se, but "the 'painstaking hermeneutic' of actual Canadian conditions." I do not presume faith, but move toward it.

It is Baum's articulation of the vantage point provided by the preferential option that appeals: "The preferential option inevitably discloses the ambiguity of culture, brings out its political content, reveals the extent to which culture protects the dominant structures and uncovers the more hidden symbols in the culture that nourish the dream of an alternative, more humane society."[57]

The murderous act of the Montreal Massacre was devastating. Equally disturbing for many women who looked to the news for information was "the vast orchestration and channeling of interpretations into nonthreatening territories." "More than at any other time in my life," wrote Margot Lacroix, "I felt the seemingly inexorable weight of this patriarchal society's safety mechanisms."[58] The cultural mainstream, "mediated by various cultural institutions, including the mass media," disguises structures of oppression.[59] Lacroix's comment refers to a tendency to disguise, to mask conflict, and veil dissent. It is an observation from the underside. The ambivalent position of belonging and not-belonging allows women to become perceptive critics of the social order.[60] "Truly to know society ... is to recognize it in its contradictions."[61] If we are to know society, we must listen to those who live its contradictions.

Dorothy Smith

The principles articulated by Baum, which provide a rationale for a turn to the Montreal Massacre, also prepare the ground for a presentation of the work of Dorothy Smith. Theologians choose among various social science approaches in accordance with their theological perspective.[62] Because my theological approach begins with solidarity with women, I choose to consider the work of a feminist sociologist who begins there also. Smith's interests are funnelled into two major lines of inquiry: "first, into what it means to explore the social from the site of women's experience and beginning therefore with an experiencing and embodied subject, and second, into the social organization of the objectified knowledges that are essential constituents of the relations of ruling of contemporary capitalism."[63] Both these lines of thought grew out of Smith's unease with conventional sociological practices, the objectifying methodologies of which deny the speech of women's experience by substituting the categories of an impersonal discourse for those of women.[64] Of her training in sociology, which began at the London School of Economics and continued at the University of California at Berkeley, Smith says: "I learned not to think about individual people; I learned how to use a language that withdrew attention from the fact that there were real people around in the world. I learned to think of properties of social structures." She adds: "I felt the problem that I was confronting was one of overcoming this way in which sociology seemed naturally to neglect the immediate world that I was part of, the world that I went home to.... This world that I went home to didn't have a place in what the sociologists had to say."[65]

A women's studies course taught at the University of British Columbia in the early 1970s provided her with the opportunity to begin thinking in a systematic way about the "problem" of sociology. It included the matter of the exclusion of women, but there was more than that. She writes:

> As I thought about it, it became clear to me it was more of a problem than just women not being there in the various ways that women are not there—that they were not mentioned, that they weren't thought of, that the whole way in which the field was conceptualized simply didn't include women.... I saw that this conceptual organization that I'd learned to think with ... put me in a particular relationship to the world: it created a way of looking at the world as if one were placed outside it.... [The business of sociology] was to create a position from which to think about the world, to look out on it as a ruler surveying the territory of his rule.[66]

"Established sociology has objectified a consciousness of society and social relations that 'knows' them from the standpoint of their ruling and from the standpoint of men who do the ruling."[67] The familiar categories of sociology, mental illness, violence, juvenile delinquency, and the like have "come into being as integral constituents and products of the bureaucratic, legal, and professional operations of this apparatus" and in terms of their concerns.[68] "Issues are formulated because they are administratively relevant, not because they are significant first in the experience of those who live them."[69] It is not simply or only that issues of relevance to those who manage predominate. Sociological practices subsume lives and then organize for administration what has been subsumed into something that would not be readily recognizable by those who have had the work of sociology done to them. "The traditional methods of sociology objectify the social process, eliminating from its representation the presence of subjects as active in bringing a concerted social world into being."[70]

One of the means by which this is accomplished is through linguistic conjuring. All you have to do is to find a verb, dress it up, leave out the subject, convert it to a noun, and you have a new social phenomenon: aggression, violence, interaction, motivation, alienation.[71] The presence of subjects is suspended, and agency is reattributed from subjects to social phenomena. Smith refers to the sociological practices of writing texts that subdue people's experiences by substituting abstractions for human actions as ideological practices. From Marx she develops an understanding of ideology that includes in its definition those ideas and symbols that serve to endorse and protect the interests of a particular group, but she expands on this. An ideological practice is "that which creates a rupture in the relation between the forms of thought as the practices of a discourse and the activities of actual individuals that are expressed in them."[72] Concepts become a barrier rather than a point of departure. "Domestic violence" is a case in point. The concept masks the direction of violence; it obliterates the actual living individuals in their actual contexts of action. "There are no agents; the presence of men and women, of men, women, and children as subjects in these relations of violence are suppressed." The concept localizes the context of violence. "The representatives of the state do not do violence.... Who acts and how disappears. We cannot see what is going on."[73] This kind of conceptual conjuring has real consequences. The absorption of human agency restricts the possibility of agency. Theoretical practices which remove individual experience and activity as a locus of agency in social reality "restrict [our] efforts to see [our] activities and experiences as information about how the world is and how it might be."[74]

Smith identifies and opposes thought constructs and analytical categories crafted to abolish or deny the presence of the human. In effect, she identifies and opposes a particular manifestation of social sin, although she would not describe it as such. By identifying the sites and processes of oppression and exclusion—the actual social practices and relations by which knowledge is organized to exclude the actualities of people's lives[75]— the agents of sin are made visible. The processes of exclusion are not amorphous; they cannot be attributed to unfindable and therefore unchangeable forces and factors. There is no "outbreak of sexism virus," as the *Globe and Mail* characterized attacks on women students at the University of Alberta, for instance, no free-floating thing with an existence of its own, but only real people's speech and actions.[76]

Because "our means of knowing and speaking of ourselves and our world are written for us by men who occupy a special place in it,"[77] there is a rift between women's experience and "the social forms of thought available in which to express it and make it actionable," a "disjunction between how women find and experience the world ... and the concepts and theoretical schemes available to think about it in."[78] The recognition of this disjuncture, and the realization that it might be otherwise, breached Smith's relation to the discipline: "The thinking and investigating I've been doing ... originated in the dramatic moment when I discovered in my own life that there was a standpoint from which a woman might know the world very differently from the way knowledge has already claimed it," she explains.[79] "The moment of rupture ... directed me toward a rewriting of the methods of knowing that I worked with."[80] This best locates Smith's appeal for me. I have been fascinated, filled with angry energy, by the recognition of a line of fault, a chasm, between my experiences and understandings of the world and those conveyed in the classroom or by the media. Smith does not rest with the identification of points of rupture. With other feminists, and in a systematic and compelling way, she deliberately takes up the disjuncture as an enterprise.[81]

An attempt to define an alternative has been at the heart of much of Smith's work since the early 1970s, an attempt to do it differently, to think differently about society and social relations, and to think from the standpoint of women rather than of men.[82] Smith's alternative explores the everyday world from the perspective of women, providing descriptions and analyses of that world so that we might better understand "the ways in which women's lives *shape and are shaped by* the social order."[83] She states: "I think we can imagine a sociology that might reach out to understand the kind of social relations in which our lives are embedded so that we could see how things work, the way they're organized, the way power relations are structured, how things are put together so that they happen to us in the ways they do."[84]

No small undertaking. "I thought I would rewrite sociological methods of thinking and writing its texts," Smith explains. "It would be a knowledge and analytic capacity written from ... a standpoint outside the textually mediated conversations of the relations of ruling, and situated in the particularities of the everyday worlds of our immediate experience."[85] It would "not insist that we put aside aspects of our experience of what we know by virtue of the living we do in an ordinary everyday way in an ordinary everyday world."[86] It would be a sociology providing "for sub-jects' means of grasping the social relations organizing the worlds of their experience"—how it happens to us as it does.[87]

Smith begins with what is absent from conventional sociological con-ceptions—the standpoint of women. This does not mean "trying to find an experience that is general to all women and setting that up to govern our relevances."[88] "Women are variously located in society. Our situations are much more various than the topics we recognize somewhat stereotyp-ically as women's topics would suggest."[89] Smith's concern is not to obscure this heterogeneity, but "to develop a sociology from the standpoint of sub-jects located materially and in particular places."[90] Inquiry defined by the problematic of the everyday world addresses the problem of how we are related to the worlds in which we live.[91] The everyday world is neither transparent nor obvious; its features are intimately known, the determi-nations of its features largely unknown. Rendering the everyday world problematic instructs us to "look for the 'inner' organization generating its ordinary features, its orders and disorders, its contingencies and con-ditions, and to look for that inner organization in the externalized and abstracted relations of economic processes and of the ruling apparatus in general."[92]

The method of this feminist sociology begins in an actual situation and explores the relations that organize it.[93] There are some assumptions about the world in this. "We do suppose that there is a world that can be described: that this world has determinate socially constituted features which are the stable production of members."[94] For example, because the world has determinate features, it is possible to "reach behind" individ-ual personal relations, such as those in a particular family, to a matrix of wider relations. "In back of the personal relations of women and men in the familial context is an economic and political process which provides the conditions, exigencies, opportunities, powers and weaknesses in terms of which the interactional process goes on."[95] Those economic and polit-ical processes impact and shape the stories of men and women in the familial context, but in differing ways. The same political processes organ-ize the world differently for different persons. "The object of our inquiry is the social relations establishing the matrices of such differences. And these social relations are real."[96]

For the sociologist, the particular case is the point of entry into a larger social and economic process.[97] She seeks the social relations that form the matrix of an individual's world—not her consciousness, feelings, and perceptions. Giving women speech is an important component of Smith's methodology, so an individual's consciousness and perceptions begin the process of inquiry.[98] But Smith wants more than the sharing of experiences. She wants a systematic knowledge of society developed from the standpoint of women.[99] The question is not "what is our experience?" but rather "how is our experience organized?"[100] "In dissecting the anatomy of power relations that organize women's lives, the researcher can lay bare and make public for women the precise contours and working of their oppression."[101]

Beverly Harrison writes that "When a social theory helps people experience their presumed private troubles as actually grounded in the way the social world works, that theory is theologically and morally apt."[102] Smith would insist that hers is a method, not a theory, and I suspect she would be indifferent to whether or not it could be considered "theologically apt," but it does conform to Beverly Harrison's criteria for being so considered. The method Smith proposes begins from a particular site in the world, *is* interested, and intends an explanation of the everyday world "in terms of actual socially organized practices ('how it actually works')."[103] It makes connections between "private troubles" and the way the social world works.

Smith's second line of inquiry progresses from a critique of the alienating practices of sociology. Smith explains: "As I began to see the objectified methods of thinking and writing texts characteristic of the social sciences, I also began to see them as integral to that great complex of relations and apparatuses of ruling at work in contemporary society."[104]

> Contemporary society has a special and distinctive organization specialized as management, administration, professional organization, cultural and scientific discourses, and mass media. These interlaced and intercoordinated relations [Smith has] called the *relations of ruling*, for two reasons: one is that they actually do the work of organizing and coordinating the overall societal process—they rule—and the second is that the mass of people play no part in how they operate other than as audience, consumer, marginally as voters, or as workers subordinated to their internal managerial or administrative processes.[105]

People's lives are accommodated to the systems set up to control them, that fit their troubles into standardized terms by which they can be recognized and made actionable within bureaucratic, professional, or managerial modes.[106] This process is encountered in the ordinary and pervasive aspects of our daily lives: in traffic tickets, passports, grades, news programs, statistics, "and the other multifarious forms in which people's doings are translated into marks on paper or images on film."[107]

This line of inquiry is concerned with "the practices of thinking and writing that convert what people experience into forms of knowledge in which people as subjects disappear and in which their perspectives on their own experience are transposed and subdued by the magisterial forms of objectifying discourse."[108] Inquiry begins with the texts produced by bureaucracies, texts that are to be explored as we know them. Each of us has written reports, filled out questionnaires, and attempted to accommodate the actualities of our lives to the forms that govern them: the proposals for grant money, the job applications, the tax forms. Smith's outline of the insider's materialism requires that we make conscious use of our unexamined knowledge as a resource for our investigation of relations of ruling mediated by texts.[109] This line of inquiry addresses "the conceptual practices used by professionals (researchers, policy makers) to provide us with ways of understanding and organizing our experiences of the world." Professionals are obliged to actively define issues in accordance with organizational practices and assign them to the appropriate professional jurisdictions.[110] The realities of peoples' lives are recycled into forms admissible to and recognizable in particular institutional settings—a practice that packages and diminishes those lives.

Much of Smith's work has involved an examination of the techniques and structures by which women are excluded, silenced, or subordinated within the practice of sociology in particular and in the larger context of the practices of the ruling apparatus. Many of these techniques and structures were operative in the presentation of and responses to the Montreal Massacre. Using Smith as guide, I want "to offer something like a map or diagram of the swarming relations in which our lives are enmeshed so that we can find our ways better among them."[111]

Gregory Baum and Dorothy Smith

Gregory Baum and Dorothy Smith are contemporaries, both Canadians born elsewhere, who deal with many of the same questions from differing perspectives. In his work, Gregory Baum explores the relation of theology to the social sciences, to society, and to the struggle for justice.[112] In hers, Dorothy Smith considers the links between sociology and the ruling apparatus, the disjuncture between objectified accounts and particular lives, and the possibilities for "a systematic knowledge of society developed from the standpoint of women."[113] Both see connections between analysis and commitment, between our personal lives and the forces shaping them, and between our understanding of the world and the possibility of change within it.

Elements of Smith's sociology can be seen in each of Baum's three theses. Thesis I states that theology must address its historical context. The aim of Smith's project is to explore the everyday world from the standpoint of women, "providing for women analyses, descriptions, and understandings of their situation, of their everyday world and its determinations in the larger socioeconomic organization."[114] The intent is "to discover and ... understand the objective social, economic, and political relations which shape and determine women's oppression in this kind of society."[115] According to Thesis II, scientific and theological considerations influence the choice among sociological approaches. Smith's work fulfils Baum's criteria for scientific inquiry. Its express purpose is to illuminate connected phenomena and to explain relations hitherto obscure.[116] It uncovers structures of domination—the social, economic, and political relations which shape and determine women's oppression—and puts into determinate relation the researcher and those participating in the research project.[117] But choosing a paradigm is not purely an exercise in scientific rationality.[118] "The truth of a theory is not dependent on the application of certain methodological principles and rules, but on its potential to orient the process of praxis towards progressive emancipation and humanization."[119] Baum favours "a sociology that aims at justice, fosters emancipation, and promotes humanity."[120] Smith's project aims at changing conditions of limitation, fosters an enlarged capacity to see, and promotes women as subjects.

Smith and Baum are not in complete accord, however, particularly regarding the approach advocated for best understanding the world in which we live. In his second thesis, Baum discusses "three types of social theories that present a sociology of evil applicable to contemporary society."[121] In order to establish the point that not every sociological theory is equally appropriate for analyzing the social context, he assesses the implications of each and argues that a conflict sociology is most appropriate for understanding contemporary evil. He presents three theories, chooses one, and shows how that one "works." The approach recommended by Dorothy Smith is different: "If we were to aim at a sociology for Canadians, i.e. one that addressed itself to the explication of the social determinations of the various worlds of experience contained within this political and economic frame, then we would have to have a sociology which begins just there rather than from the conceptual traditions of a discourse among sociologists, whether Canadian or not, whether critical or complacent, radical or conservative."[122] Smith's approach does not look for a theory to describe society, but looks at society directly. To understand our social world "we must have a method of arriving at an adequate description and analysis of how it actually works. Our methods cannot rest in problems of validating theories, which to a large extent have become procedures for deciding among different formalized 'opinions' about the world."[123]

It is relatively simple to insert Smith's project into Baum's third thesis, that "in the Canadian context theology must be based on preferential solidarity."[124] Her sociology stands with women who are outside the relations of ruling, and investigates the world from that perspective. The standpoint has both hermeneutical and emancipatory dimensions: the world is viewed from the position of women within it, and the subject of research is "she whose grasp of the world from where she stands is enlarged thereby."[125] But again, there are substantial differences in the approach of the two scholars. When Baum refers to "the preferential option" he points to solidarity for and with "the poor," "the depressed and dependent sector of society," the "victims." Referring to the poor, oppressed, and marginalized as victims is problematic. It is a designation which masks the experience and agency of those so called, and separates "us" from "them." Smith takes a stand with those who are largely subordinate within the ruling apparatus, but her formulation does not identify women as victims. Public consciousness of widespread violence against women is a good and necessary thing, but "victimologies have their limitations. They tend to create the false impression that women have only been victims, that they have never successfully fought back, that women cannot be effective social agents on behalf of themselves or others. But … women have always resisted male domination."[126] Smith creates a point of departure from which to consider both the structures of domination and the paths of resistance. This stands as a corrective to the tendency to describe too narrowly the reality of those who suffer under, and resist, the burden of unjust social structures.

The coincidence of concerns in the work of Baum and Smith does not imply the conflation of theology and sociology. Sociology is the systematic study of social organizations, institutions, and relations. Its tools, methodologies, and analyses are frequently used by contextual and liberation theologians around the globe, but they do not *replace* theology with sociology. "It is impossible to find a simple formula relating theology and sociology because neither branch of knowledge is a unified human science operating out of a clearly defined set of principles and following a universally recognized methodology," Baum states.[127] There are differences in starting point and purpose, however. Theology includes at the outset a guiding vision that is compelled by faith. Both Anselm's eleventh-century definition of theology as "faith seeking understanding," and my reversal of it, "understanding seeking faith," place faith at the heart of theology (although our definitions of "faith" would no doubt diverge widely). The purpose of theology is to reflect on, and further, the reaches of the sacred. That takes place here through an examination of violations to life and a call to challenge those acts, structures, and processes that are life-denying.

In the chapters that follow I apply to the Montreal Massacre, as a particular and revelatory "moment," resources garnered from Smith and Baum, making observable some of the structures that underlie accounts of, arguments over, and responses to it. This is actualized through the conceptual application of elements of Smith's sociological critique and methodology (particularly her critique of ideology, her materialist method, and her elaboration of the standpoint of women), to the construction of and debates over the massacre (as they are available to me through the media, both dominant and alternative, and in the responses of popular groups), precisely as a theological exercise. In chapter 2 I use Dorothy Smith's approach to the world and her understanding of it to explore the institutions and narratives engaged in the presentation of the massacre. The undercutting of feminist political analyses and the depoliticization of issues as they are channelled through regulatory institutions are particular areas of inquiry. Smith's investigation, both into what it means to explore the social from the site of women's experiences and into the conceptual practices that are essential constituents of the relations of ruling, constructs a vantage point from which the workings of power can be traced.[128] Chapter 3 articulates more explicitly the theological implications of the analysis developed in the previous chapter. By opening up the complex of relations that shape women's oppression in Canadian society, the analysis makes possible a more specific naming of the meaning and the value issues at stake. In other words, it makes possible a more specific, and adequate, *theological* naming. Chapter 4 shifts the angle of vision and considers a variety of creative responses to the murders in Montreal as manifestations of a "spirituality of resistance."

"One's theology has to be contextual, concrete, analyze the various historical forces and their respective visions that define North America, and enter into solidarity with movements committed to emancipation," says Gregory Baum.[129] Theology must analyze and critically reflect upon its historical context.[130] So instructed, I turn, with Smith and Baum, to a day indelibly etched into the minds of many Canadians.

2: How Does It Happen to Us as It Does?

December, 1989. In *Maclean's* it read like this: "For 20 horrific minutes last week, a quiet young man named Marc Lépine stalked female students in a Montreal university engineering school—killing 14 of them before turning his rifle on himself. It was Canada's worst mass murder—and among the worst in North American history. And it set off a national wave of mourning and revived a debate over violence against women."

From that same story:

> At first, they viewed it as a prank,... in keeping with the festive spirit that marked the second-last day of classes at the University of Montreal's Ecole Polytechnique.
> ... He entered the classroom slowly a few minutes past 5 on a bitterly cold afternoon.
> ... He asked the women to move to one side of the room and ordered the men to leave.
> ... "You're all a bunch of feminists, and I hate feminists," Lépine shouted.
> ... Six of the women were shot dead. Over the course of the next 20 minutes, the young man methodically stalked the cafeteria, the classrooms and the corridors of the school, leaving a trail of death and injury in his wake.
> ... All of the dead—except for the gunman himself—were women.

The story did not end, of course, with details of the rampage: "in four separate locations scattered around three floors of the six-story structure"; nor with the price and destructive power of the rifle used: "the Ruger Mini-14 semiautomatic rifle ... can hold up to 50 rounds of ammunition.... And at a cost of between $560 and $650, it is one of the most popular rifles in Canada"; nor with profiles of Lépine: "a 25-year-old-man who repeatedly failed to achieve his ambitions in work—and with women"; nor even with the puzzlement of prominent persons: "the Prime Minister … asked a hushed House of Commons: 'Why such violence in a society that considers itself civilized and compassionate?'"[1] Elsewhere, the story continued with reports of threats to other women: a voice over the phone, whispering "Marc is not alone"; with efforts to de-gender the killings: "you shouldn't say fourteen women were killed; they were fourteen *people*"; and with a rush to reassure us that the massacre was the incomprehensible act of a madman.

For some of us, the story also included the full page Birks advertisement in *Maclean's* placed opposite a picture of a wounded woman from the shooting, lying in a pool of blood—an ad which featured a woman's mouth and pearled neck and read: "Knock 'em dead!" It included the elimination of core financing to eighty women's groups a few weeks after the massacre, and finance minister Michael Wilson's assertion that it was "absolutely outrageous" to mention one in connection with the other.[2] It included the fact that in 1989, 119 women died of domestic violence in Canada.

From a sociological perspective, Dorothy Smith asks: "How does it happen to us as it does? How is the world in which we act and suffer put together?"[3] These are also theological questions, questions about our present, about our future, about sinfulness and despair, and about the possibilities for change. These are the questions that compel the analysis developed here. Using Dorothy Smith's method, her proposal for "a way of seeing, from where we actually live, into the powers, processes and relations that organize and determine the everyday context of that seeing,"[4] I begin to track various of those powers and processes. Through Gregory Baum's understanding of critical theology, a dimension of which is turning to redemptive, critical use the abstractions and categories of sociology,[5] I "enter" the analysis developed into theological discourse. Taking up my wit and anguish, I begin to map a way through the wilderness.

Years after the murders at Ecole Polytechnique, the echoes of gunshots still reverberate. December 6, 1989, is firmly lodged in the Canadian collective conscience. A decade afterward, as the turn of the millennium approached, the Montreal Massacre was named by *Maclean's* magazine as one of the decisive moments to shape Canada in the previous 100 years.[6] It has provided the opportunity for endless speculation, the occasion for countless articles. Whether it is considered a consequence of inadequate gun laws or a monstrous instance of ongoing violence against women, the Montreal Massacre has become, for many, a cultural and political symbol. I want to approach it differently, not only as a symbol but also as a discursive opening. To the degree that any symbol points to a larger reality, the massacre *can* be taken as symbolic of the real or threatened violence many women in this society face. However, "symbol" can imply detachment and elevation. I do not want to "raise up" the massacre, but to explore its embeddedness, to approach it as a window into established and ongoing political and social relations and processes which shape our lives. This shifts the discourse from opinions and arguments over what the massacre did or did not *represent,* to an examination of the relations in which our lives are embedded.

The complex of relations that shape our lives is precisely that—complex. Any attempt to map a way through them will be partial at best. My focus is on the immediate aftermath of the murders and two years subsequent (1989–91), when a number of significant initiatives were launched. I also make frequent references to analyses developed since 1989 and explore various anniversary events. The tenth anniversary, in particular, was a time for widespread national reflection on the murders and the changes implemented since. As I write, we have marked the sixteenth anniversary, and once more Canadians have broached questions about how far we have come and how far we have left to go. This book partakes in those discussions.

A Line of Fault

The murders horrified me. They did not surprise. For me and for many others the massacre raised memories of many other acts of violence directed toward women on a daily basis. It was not a revelation but rather a remembering, as Sylvie Gagnon, one of the survivors, described her own response in a documentary interview.[7] It occasioned a retelling—or the telling for the first time—of other acts of violence known or suffered. The gunman's actions that fateful day were merciless and monstrous, but not incomprehensible. They were all too comprehensible, in fact. Women were targeted and killed, as women are targeted and killed with great frequency. Does a number take it out of the realm of the mundane and into madness? Even fourteen?

As I watched the television and read the newspapers, another kind of horror set in. There was an unbridgeable gap between my inchoate analysis and that most often made available in the dominant media. A struggle over meaning was being engaged. In the days following, the experts consulted were primarily psychologists, not feminists, which served to focus the inquiry on the inner workings of one man's mind, not the broader world of gender politics. Both the presentation of the massacre in the mainstream media—the floundering for analysis, conflicts over meaning, its construction as incomprehensible—and the information conveyed therein about the responses of various groups and persons—the police, government representatives, and school officials—filled me with dismay. That this experience was not mine alone became readily apparent in conversations with friends in the days after the massacre and was also a recurring theme among women writing about December 6 in alternative media or as letters to editors.[8] The purpose here is not to share the feelings or document the sharing but rather to consider the social relations that generated this line of fault.[9] Dorothy Smith directs us to "reach behind" individual experiences to the matrix of wider relations that shape and condition those experiences. I take up her approach to the world and her understanding of it to uncover some of the forms and processes by which the massacre was presented, such that all the material left us weary, and did not satisfy.[10]

Problematic: The Organization of Power

The standpoint of women is grounded in women's experience, located outside the ruling apparatus, in the everyday world. It "situates the inquirer in the site of her bodily existence and in the local actualities of her working world."[11] Taking this literally, I begin where I am, surrounded by books, articles, and newspaper clippings, a decade and a half after the massacre, trying to understand. The insider's materialism Smith puts forward, and which is adopted here, begins in local actualities and explores, from the inside, the relations that tie the local to the generalizing relations that organize it. It "is intended to deepen and expand our access to the actualities of our lives and what we are caught up in without knowing it." She welcomes its application: "the techniques of analysis and the concepts are there for your use. Feel free."[12] I do. Smith directs "our gaze toward the ongoing co-ordering of activities that brings our world into being, toward how ... it is 'accomplished.'"[13] So instructed, I consider here how the massacre was taken up—in the mainstream media; officially, by the police, coroner, and government representatives; and by women critical of these processes—as available in the many words that surround me.

There is an undeniable, and ambiguous, privileging of the published word in such an approach. I have no access to the voices and experiences of those who have no access to publication. The irony does not escape me. I critique the relations of ruling while being a marginal part of them as I enter a horrifying event into academic discourse. My relationship to these texts is also ambiguous. I rely on them for information about how the world is constructed: about police responses on the day of the shooting, the coroner's report, the reaction and responses of various government representatives, and so on. I read through them into the social relations producing and sustaining them; they convey information about the world and also traces of its organization. The product of the practices and activities of persons in institutionalized settings, texts reflect those practices and activities, and the social world in which they are accomplished.

I am in partnership with the texts. We arrive at a knowledge of the world by extending what we already know as practitioners toward the development of a systematic consciousness of society and social relations.[14] I rely on my own knowledge of how the world is constituted, the texts of others who have commented on the massacre, and Smith, whose work contributes to both the structure and content of the analysis developed. The institutions and structures that shape and overpower our lives are myriad. Smith deals with particular sites and processes of exclusion, starting with the exclusion of women from the making of knowledge and culture, examining not so much the active and often violent repression of women as the silencing that results from steady institutional processes. To this context of the Montreal Massacre, I transfer various of Smith's conceptualizations, points of analysis, and her understanding of the way Canadian society is constituted. Although I rely on a sociologist, this investigation is not sociological. I am not formally implementing the kind of sociological project Smith proposes, but rather following the pattern and purpose of her method by making a line of fault the starting point for analysis and examining this line of fault to see how it is organized. More substantially, I rely on her for explication of how this silencing happens as it does, and the consequences to women of how it happens.

By adopting and adapting Smith's method to examine various ways in which the massacre was taken up, I am shifting the focus from the actual event to the naming of the event. I am not after "why he did it," although that question does constitute much of the debate that took place in the press and elsewhere. He said quite clearly why he did it. Neither am I particularly interested in the man, although again, the man, his personal history, and psychological state were matters of much speculation. I *am* interested in the various responses to the massacre: its presentation, characterization, and the ways in which it was acted upon, or not. The fact of and responses to the massacre provide a point of entry into patterns of exercising power in our society, and I want to understand them better.[15]

Backdrop: A Struggle over Meaning

To report, as did *Maclean's*, that the massacre "revived a debate over violence against women" is an understatement. Rarely before in Canadian history has this "debate" been so widely or passionately engaged. A contest over meaning ensued, a struggle over whose knowledge would define it. It was played out most explicitly in the pages of local newspapers: on editorial pages, in commentary and opinion pieces, in interviews, and in reports of pranks and threats. But it was also a struggle that had been structured prior to its visibility on any printed page. The massacre was examined professionally, by mass-murder experts, government officials, policing agents, and the coroner, among others, and articulated according to the interests of their respective domains. The struggle was played out by means of the emphases, conceptualizations, and concepts used to describe the assassinations (and the world in which they happened), and the effort to "work it up" to fit the conceptual framework of this jurisdiction or that. Many of those who participated in this struggle would perhaps not understand it so, considering it merely the practical and conceptual work of reporting, policing, or psychologizing. But a struggle it was—for meaning, for definition, and for a way to respond. Like many political struggles, this was about representation and the framing of questions, and there was nothing neutral or arbitrary about it. There is an intimate link between the understanding and definition of a problem and the understanding and definition of its resolution. It is a struggle that was and is "theologically charged." Concerns about the construction of meaning, and the naming of good and evil, are essential theological concerns.

The Social Construction of Knowledge: The Media Presentation

The socially organized production and transmission of ideas and images
deprives women of access to the means to reflect on, formulate, and
express their experience and their situation.[16]

— Dorothy Smith, 1975

In the National Film Board production *After the Montreal Massacre*, Sylvie
Gagnon relates her experience of being wounded and leaving the campus
to go to a friend's house to talk, to tell someone what had happened. "A
madman.... He shot me." At her friend's expression of disbelief, Gagnon
countered with "come and watch the TV." Reflecting afterward about the
exchange, Gagnon had this to say: "It's strange, eh, when you live through
an extremely intense experience and to validate it I had to refer to TV so
people would believe me. I heard the full story on TV at the same time as
everyone else."[17]

Media images have authority comparable to the authority previously
reserved for religious teachings.[18] They have become normative: if it
appears on television, it "really happened"; what happens in silence does
not exist. They are all-pervasive. As Smith notes, "The scope and inten-
siveness of the production of the social forms of thought is greater in this
type of society than in any previously known." They are "the forms given
to people to understand what is happening to them,... the means we are
given to examine our experience, our needs and anxieties."[19] And, like
religious teachings, they are produced by certain groups of people in certain positions. On the surface, what is read or seen may appear simply as
informative data speaking of the world beyond;[20] however, this is merely
appearance. "It is misleading to treat news ... as arising in a simple relation in which information given on one side is received by the other."[21]
"The facticity, content and structure of news [is] an organizational accomplishment,... [standing] in a far from simple relation to events it [claims]
to represent."[22]

What was accomplished in the media presentation of the Montreal
Massacre? I have no access to the inner workings of newsrooms or television studios, but I do have access to what was produced there, to the
work of other women who have commented on the media presentation,
and to Dorothy Smith's analyses of ideological structures and of how

women are excluded. Even a brief survey of the media coverage in the days following the massacre uncovers ongoing practices and relations which exclude in fact and mystify in effect.[23]

Many of us remember where we were when we first heard that a gunman had targeted women at an engineering school in Montreal and remember also the shock, the not wanting to believe, and the first disjointed reports on the news that night. Among the headlines the next day: "Campus Massacre: Gunman kills 14 women before shooting himself" (*Gazette*, Dec. 7, 1989); "Un tireur fou abat 14 femmes" (*La Presse*, Dec. 7, 1989); "Man in Montreal kills 14 women" (*Globe and Mail*, Dec. 7, 1989). With these, the barrage of reports, responses, and speculation began. The Montreal *Gazette*'s coverage was typical, if more extensive than other papers. On its first pages were details released by the police, the experience of several men on the site, and the responses of prominent figures. Information was sketchy, gathered largely from students or teachers present when the shooting began. "I heard the gunman say: 'I want the women,'" one male student was quoted as saying. "We took off running," said another.[24] From the police came details about the make of the gun, the number of shots fired, the location of the fourteen slain, and the suicide note in which the gunman blamed women for his failures in life. Montreal mayor Jean Doré and the director of the Ecole Polytechnique, both in France at the time, were called for comment. "The act of a maniac," one said. "One can imagine such a thing happening elsewhere, but not here," said the other.[25] In the banner article on the front page, fifteen men were identified by name and quoted, among them students, police, and university representatives, and prominent persons. One unidentified woman was quoted: "My daughter's in there."[26]

There were a number of accompanying articles. One described student journalists barricading themselves in a room. Another gave a chronology of terror: At 4:30 this, at 5:15 that, blood here and there. A third listed the most bloody incidents in Canada's history, noting that the massacre "eclipses by far Canada's worst shootings."[27] It was the third worst in North American history; these too were listed. A fourth described how a couple's evening celebration was turned into a nightmare. Yet another related the reaction of members of the National Assembly who expressed their shock and sympathy. "I don't think we could remain unmoved by an act so murderous and incomprehensible," said Parti Québécois deputy house leader François Gendron.[28] Prominent on the front page of the

Gazette was the picture of one of the murdered women slumped in a chair in the cafeteria while in the background a man removed Christmas decorations.

The *Globe and Mail* was more restrained, its large-scale photo a picture of a woman in tears at a candlelight vigil in Montreal, but the basic content was the same: details, interviews, and a list of "some of the worst one-day massacres in Canadian history."[29] A story, "the story," was constructed from innumerable details and truncated interviews with survivors and dignitaries. In an article titled "La mascarade médiatique," Myriame El Yamani, a sociologist who analyzed the immediate media coverage, comments on the limitations of this kind of reporting: "La narration, dans la pratique journalistique,… permet de décrire sans avoir à expliquer, de créer une histoire, en occultant le contexte socio-historique et politique dans lequel l'événement s'est produit. Les seuls éléments de contextualisation que les six quotidiens considérés reproduiront seront une dépêche d'agence de presse, faisant une rétrospective, dans le temps et dans le mond, de ce type de forfaits sanglants."[30]

From the outset, "what it meant" became an issue. Barbara Frum on *The Journal*, responding to interviewees who related the murders to the broader spectrum of violence against women, claimed persistently that "we should not focus on the fact that women were the targets; we should see the tragedy as something that 'diminished all of us'—men and women alike, and by extension, all equally."[31] It was a crime against humanity, not women.

El Yamini notes that on December 8, commentary from experts was highlighted in the newspapers: "Le 8 décembre: les médias continuent à produire une myriade de récits éphémères qui font apparaître l'histoire comme une production ingouvernable d'événements et surtout qui ne souffre pas le doute ou la remise en question. On entre alors dans la stratégie du psychologisme intensif…. C'est à ce moment-là qu'entrent en scène les expert(e) de tout acabit: psychologues, psychiatres, médecins, prêtres, juristes … etc.[32]" The headline story in the *Globe and Mail* focused on an intelligent but troubled Lépine. Two story lines were evident, lines that would be amplified and elaborated in the days and weeks to follow. One was based on bio-psycho-psychiatric explanations: Lépine was schizophrenic or had paranoid tendencies. The second centred on his personal history, offering a socio-criminological explanation for the crime: he was beaten as a child; he was abandoned by his father; he had trouble with women; he was rejected by the army. Both story lines isolated and made exceptional the murderer and his act.[33] A second article, "Quebec mourns slaying of women at university," described flags at half mast and teary-eyed students at the Ecole Polytechnique. The description of a candlelight vigil focused on discordant moments: a scuffle "as a group of women tried to prevent a man from addressing the crowd," and "boos and catcalls from male and female students" in response to one woman "who told the crowd that the slaughter 'shows the extreme of hatred from men which women must live with in our society.'"[34] This too would be a recurrent theme in the days and weeks ahead: trouble is where women are vocal.

A later page of the *Globe and Mail* was completely devoted to the "Aftermath in Montreal." It consisted of articles on gun control, police responses on December 6, comments from experts on mass murder, a description of a vigil in Toronto with quotations from a number of women connecting the massacre to other instances of violence, and the killer's purchase of his gun. Only two articles addressed the gendered character of the murders. Elsewhere, the *Globe and Mail*'s editorial and two opinion pieces considered the massacre in the context of ongoing violence against women: "the horrifying executions … emerge from a social context and cannot be disowned."[35] In the *Toronto Star*, Michele Landsberg warned that we deceive ourselves to call this crime the act of a madman. "Violent women-hating is a daily truth."[36] The weight of these pieces is offset by the fact that these are opinion columns. As a fact among other facts, the act had already been set within the context of other mass murders. Coverage of vigils across the country was similarly circumscribed, according to Lee Lakeman, a member of a collective that operated a Vancouver women's shelter. She noted that vigils were often "characterized as 'spontaneous' gatherings, effectively hiding the people and groups behind them. Voiceless and, apparently, leaderless, women were posited as fearful and passive." Female voices heard by the public were largely limited to emotional identification with the victims. "In the coverage, there are not details about the organizers and the speeches." Instead, women are asked: "Does this make you more afraid?"[37]

On December 9, more of everything. In the *Globe and Mail* were interviews with wounded students, details of Lépine's life, and editorial and opinion pieces on gun control, on the danger of "the self-interested hyperbole that mass slaughter encourages," and mourning the loss of "our bright and shining daughters."[38] Moving into increasing prominence was reaction against reactions to the murders that placed them in the context of men's violence against women. Joan Baril's analysis of responses to the massacre and responses to those responses provides a case in point. She addressed the backlash that centred on a decision by the Thunder Bay's Northern Women's Centre to hold a vigil for women only. The day after the murders, many people phoned the centre wanting to talk about it, among them a number of women in distress who "related the violence that had been done to them in the past. The killings had triggered off powerful emotions of fear, rage and pain." The centre decided to have a vigil for women only and also publicize two other planned public memorials. "The story made the national news. Almost all reports omitted the fact that there were two other vigil services in Thunder Bay, much less describing the Centre's involvement in [advertising] them." According to the reports, "men were 'barred,' 'denied entry' or 'not welcome.'" An alderman who said that the actions of those at the centre were "mind terrorism" was quoted by almost every major newspaper.[39] That no men called wanting to attend the service was not mentioned.

This and vigils like it became matters of public debate. Comparisons were made between Lépine's separation of men from women and women-only vigils. Men's rights became an issue: "I refuse to be told, as in Thunder Bay, that I should not be permitted a public expression of my sorrow because I am a man."[40] The response of the women's centre *to* the murders (the planning of a vigil for women), was held responsible *for* the murders. According to the Thunder Bay newspaper, "the shootings were caused by 'the divisions created in Canadian society by the mere presence of the women's movement.' By insisting on barring men from their vigil the Northern Women's Centre 'invites the very negative attitudes against women it strives to erase.'"[41] The frame of public discourse shifted away from the initial act of violence, "and onto the (in)appropriateness of the reaction by feminists," from women's pain to men's perceived loss of rights.[42]

As the official joint funeral approached, press coverage was devoted to details of the church service and the lives of the slain. The *Globe and Mail* on December 11 reported the thousands of mourners and hundreds of telegrams, along with more details of Lépine's life and the police investigation. The next day, the front page of the Montreal *Gazette* was dominated by a picture of white coffins in front of the altar of Notre Dame Basilica.

The accompanying articles described the funeral, the dignitaries in attendance, high points of the homily, and the tears. There were details of the
personal lives of the victims and moving descriptions of the shared grief
of those outside the church. These emphasized the unity among the
mourners, men and women together, and the overwhelming response of
the city, typified in this remark: "I must say Montreal has really pulled
together on this."[43] "Qui n'aura pas été ... bouleversé(e) par la prise de
vue ... du père d'une des victimes, éclatant en sanglots devant le cercueil
de sa fille?... Cette technique journalistique n'est pas gratuite; au con-
traire, elle a pour but de réduire l'indetermination du social et de ren-
forcer une conception de la société cohérente."[44]

Over the course of the next days and weeks, these "patterns" were
repeated and replayed: the surfeit of details, narration without contextu-
alization, coverage of displays of public mourning and grief that were
occasionally interrupted by the "excesses" of some women, recourse to psychological explanations, and heated debates over meaning. El Yamani's
survey of 311 articles and 183 illustrations from December 6 to January 6
found that fewer than 10 per cent were devoted to an analysis of the actual
event. Those routinely asked for analysis were mass murder experts and
psychologists; seldom consulted were feminists knowledgeable about male
violence. Using patriarchal tools of analysis, the killer became an unhappy
young man, the victim of a miserable childhood[45]—a characterization that
obscured the political nature of the attacks. By a curious turn, political
motivation was attributed not to Lépine but rather to the responses of
those women who tried to contextualize the murders differently. Feminists were accused of politicizing the murders, of taking advantage, of
using them to attack men. The designation "political" was largely restricted
to descriptions of women who were disrupting the dominant discourse and
came to mean something sinister. It is not surprising, then, that an Angus
Reid poll released three weeks after the murders reported that six in ten
Canadians believed the massacre was a random act by an insane man, having nothing to do with violence against women in general.[46]

Opinion polls are generally understood as objective reflections of
public opinion, but they might be more correctly understood as reflections
of access to power. Public opinion was informed by the media representation of the massacre, a representation that systematically excluded certain voices, pathologized the act, and drowned analysis in a sea of details.
Of course, presentations and understandings of acts of violence against

women as random and isolated were not invented in Canada in 1989; this is a well-established custom around the world, it seems. Nevertheless, the results of such a poll must be considered an accomplishment, not a simple reflection of opinion. More correctly it was a reflection of what had been accomplished prior to December 6, and also, in highly visible ways, in the days following.

Public mourning is not the usual reaction to violence against women. Such violence is most often ignored or sensationalized, depending on the victim's class, race, and attractiveness. It is eroticized in adult video games, slasher movies, rock videos, pornography, and ads.[47] It seldom occasions concerted media attention or an outpouring of public sympathy. In fact, "the sporadic and decontextualized reportage in our press of the real daily violence against women contributes to our acceptance of it as the natural state of affairs."[48] Why is it that a number, fourteen, takes the event from the mundane to the sensational? It would be hardly news at all if it were fourteen different men, in fourteen different sites, over several months. But the end result would be the same, fourteen dead. However, in this case, "we were treated to journalism reserved for great occasions: front-page colour photos, huge screaming headlines, pages full of personal stories, and photos from family photo albums."[49] Various adjustments of focus either exaggerated or diminished the act,[50] and the murders were framed as a national tragedy, a moment of madness in an otherwise civil society.

Although there was no conspiracy operative, adjustments of focus were actively produced through the concerted work of individuals.[51] According to Dorothy Smith, "Depths and complexities of the social organization of ruling interpose between local actualities and textual surfaces.... Such textual surfaces presuppose an organization of power as the concerting of people's activities and the uses of organization to enforce processes producing a version of the world that is peculiarly one-sided."[52]

And it was "peculiarly one-sided." A politically motivated murderous act was presented primarily as an isolated incident and came to be understood as such. In spite of the evidence, this view of the massacre was prevalent.[53] Does the discussion fit neatly into "either/or" terms, that is, that it was either a random act of insanity or part of a continuum of violence against women? The poll presents these two interpretations as mutually exclusive, but they are not necessarily so, as a study by Rudy Kafer and colleagues indicates. A questionnaire investigating interpretations of the murders, given at three Canadian universities, revealed a complex understanding of them. The majority of students agreed with *both* positions, that they were a product of sexism in society, *and* that they were random and unpredictable. Such analysis is apparent in Pauline Greenhill's examination of massacre-inspired graffiti: "The argument that Lépine participated in a patriarchal structure of 'everyday' misogyny and violence against women is compelling. However, his perpetration of the massacre may be an unusually—perhaps even, we fervently hope, uniquely—violent and undoubtedly deviant example."[54] Kafer notes that "the media generally treated the randomness and sexism interpretations as though they were contradictory" and focused attention on extreme views.[55] Filmmaker Maureen Bradley refers to this kind of approach as the "constructed binary opposition of news stories." Conflict sells.

Bradley examines the way that stories are constructed in her 1995 documentary, *Reframing the Montreal Massacre*.[56] News is always framed, but the framing is often invisible. It is framed by the questions asked, the emphases made, the use of language, story placement, and the use of symbols. Bradley comments, for instance, on the fact that the fourteen murdered women were often referred to as "daughters," rendering them innocent and childlike. Although it is true that they were daughters, they were not killed because they were daughters; they were killed because they were competent women studying in a male-dominated field. The political nature of the crimes was denied. In terms of symbols, candles became an icon. A recurring image on television and in many papers was that of tearful, silent women holding candles. Solemn respect for the dead was privileged over angry responses to the murders. Bradley uses these and other examples to point out that the media is a screen of a culture; cultural values seep through in the way stories are framed. Dorothy Smith would describe this somewhat differently—that media presentations are not merely *reflections* of the culture in which they are produced, but actual *accomplishments*: "We are not talking about control of ideas in an abstract sense. Rather, we are talking about control over the means of producing and disseminating ideas and images.... The silence of those outside the apparatus is a silence in part materially organized by the preemption, indeed virtual monopoly, of communications media and the educational process as part of the ruling apparatus."[57]

The media is part of a "determinate range of social institutions forming the governing apparatus of the society," which includes government, health institutions, psychiatry, education, and the social and psychological sciences.[58] This complex "is pervasive, and pervasively interconnected."[59] Thus, prominent in the press reports of the murders are the remarks of government officials, police reports, and expert opinion. Women are largely outside this framework. It was not that women were not allowed to speak, but when they were, it was seldom as experts, depriving the "debate" of a source of specialized knowledge.[60] There is a hierarchical distinction between knowledge and experience, knowledge being more highly valued and able to confer authority where experience cannot.[61] The police and other experts spoke as knowers; their knowledge—dispassionate, abundant, and credible—served to isolate the murderous act. Women are still largely defined as persons who have no right to speak as authorities;[62] however, the *opinions* and *reactions* of women were visible in the press, especially tears and fears. An emphasis on the fear among women, rather than the responses initiated or the analyses developed, results in women being seen as victims, not agents. A focus on the emotions of potential victims detracts from the structures that make violence possible and acceptable, and detracts also from the extent of the violence: "my" fear is individual, and so very personal.

Both Lépine's act and responses to it were individualized; feminist analyses were seldom visible; there was a shift in focus from the initial violence to reactions to it; and they said over and over again that it was all incomprehensible. The version of the world visible in the media presentation of the massacre was both peculiarly one-sided and concertedly so.

An Alternative Discourse

Among women, we have created, perhaps for the first time in history, a public discourse. We established media independent of the institutionalized media of the relations of ruling, and we have also invaded, however marginally, the relations of ruling themselves.[63]
—Dorothy Smith, 1987

"The events of December 6th are both unique and general.... It was the uniqueness which was the focus of almost all initial media attention and analysis."[64] This is not the whole story, of course. Many women, and some men, organized events and developed analyses that contextualized the murders differently. Their voices, which were initially granted, at best, marginal hearing and were, at worst, misrepresented and vilified, eventually came to be more widely heard and have had an impact on reshaping the terms of the debate over the meaning of the massacre and its implications.

Gillian Walker, in a study on family violence that makes use of Smith's methodology, writes about the way dissenting voices receive a hearing.

> The process by which social reality is constructed results in there being considerable discrepancy and disjunction between the ideological forms provided for us to understand our world and our direct experience of our situation in that world. These gaps and disjunctions have, under particular historic considerations and in certain sites, allowed for the voicing of "counter-hegemonic" ideas and the taking of action by those who feel that they are not being governed by their own best interests.[65]

In the weeks, months, and now years following the Montreal Massacre there has been a massive response to the murders, a channeling of grief and outrage into action, organization, and symbolic representation. Vigils were organized, articles written, and scholarship funds and memorial bursaries established. Many women, individually or collectively, framed the murders in a way that is in striking contrast to the way examined above. The frame is larger, and the massacre seen as all too painfully comprehensible. It was an "outcome of a society where the victimization of women is not only condoned, but promoted and eroticized."[66]

I do not mean to gloss over differences among women. Every possible reaction was registered. While many women insisted that the killings must be recognized as part of a continuum of violence toward women, others refused this analysis, and reacted to what they called a feminist appropriation of the tragedy. Some women deplored a crime against humanity. Others recognized a gesture of reprisal aimed at feminists, and still others refused to engage the debate, "vowing that, until the murder of poor women, native women, runaways and prostitutes causes public outcry, they will put their energy elsewhere."[67] What is represented in this book is a line of analysis developed by feminists who viewed the massacre as part of a continuum of violence against women in general and feminists in particular. It is understood not as an isolated incident or a crime without motive, but as a crime against women. "Regardless of how extreme the act in question, it is nonetheless a coherent part of the nature of everyday violence, of which women are the primary victims."[68] That everyday violence is the very air we breathe. "And it is real. It is pervasive. It is epidemic. It saturates the society. It's very hard to make anyone notice it, because there is so much of it."[69] That there is so much violence and murder makes more murders, even fourteen at one time, anything but isolated. It was not isolated, but it was targeted. A gun was directed at these women not simply because they were women, but because they were women accused of stepping out of their place.[70] As such it was a gesture of reprisal, a political act, requiring a political analysis and political response.

That the dominant discourse *is* dominant was nowhere more apparent than within the context of this discussion. The rift between women's experience and forms of thought available to express that experience[71] was painfully evident when women tried to indicate the political nature of the massacre. Language was unavailable. Many made recourse to the analogy of racism because there is no gender equivalent. "Lépine's murders were hate crimes targeting victims by gender, not race, religion, ethnicity, or sexual orientation. When racist murders—lynchings and pogroms—occur, no one wonders whether individual perpetrators are crazy or have had bad personal experiences with African Americans and Jews.... Just as many people denied the reality of the Nazi Holocaust, most people refuse to recognize the gynocidal period in which women are living—and dying—today."[72] The history of crimes against women, "swept aside, wiped out, has only begun to be written,"[73] and in the writing the *depth* of what must change becomes apparent. It includes gender socialization, government spending priorities, the valuation of males over females, widespread pornography, the profitability of the arms trade, the glorification of violence, the wage and power gap, and the uneven distribution of wealth and property, to start. "To surpass this state of siege against women will mean no less than a transformation of the entire patriarchal system."[74]

This only begins to suggest the broad strokes of an oppositional discourse. It was voiced across the country in many and varied forms, but was seldom featured on the front pages of local newspapers. Such analysis, which appeared on occasion in mainstream news sources but most frequently in alternative magazines and newspapers, is wide-ranging and at the same time painfully specific, taking into account a too long history of violence and the name of the woman killed yesterday. It is the fruit of collective experience and engagement, not an institutional product, critical, not conciliatory, and admittedly interested.

That violence against women is an issue at all is fruit of this public discourse. It began years previous to December 6, 1989, but was much more widely engaged after that day. Its effects have been felt. On the second anniversary the *Globe and Mail* reported on a growing shift in public under-standing:

> The immediate aftermath of the mass murder was disbelief about its implications. Even a year ago, many politicians, including Quebec's min-ister in charge of the status of women, said the massacre was the work of a lone madman and not a sign of systemic and pervasive violence against women. Today, however, the massacre is widely interpreted—even at the highest political levels—as evidence of a powerful inequity between men and women in Canadian society, and as a symbol of the vio-lence women are subjected to as a result.[75]

The opinion that the massacre could only be understood as the incom-prehensible act of a madman, insofar as "incomprehensibility" can be "understood," was gradually displaced, at least in part. How? By the weight of testimony of women who simply refused to be silenced, even in the interests of their own safety, contrary to police advice. By the fact that the murderer's suicide letter which clearly stated the murderer's motivation was published a year after the murders, having been leaked to a journal-ist on his "hit list." Through the sheer weight of statistical evidence on the daily and ongoing violence against women—statistics on calls to the police, murder rates, women in shelters—evidence that came more prominently into the public domain after December 6.

While it *is* possible to refer to a changed understanding, it is also nec-essary to consider the ways in which understandings, and possibilities for change, are limited and contained as our lives and troubles are fit into the structures that govern them. I return to the first days after the massacre.

Articulation to the Social Problem Apparatus: Official Responses

In an early work examining psychiatric practices, Dorothy Smith writes that "the world that people live in and in which their troubles arise is 'entered' into the systems set up to control it by fitting them and their troubles into standardized terms and procedures under which they can be recognized and made actionable. These processes are *intrinsic* to the work-ings of … organizations. They are *essential* to the making and implement-ing of policies."[76] The experiences of people in an everyday context "are given expression in forms that articulate them to the existing practices and social relations constituting its rule."[77] So it was after the murders. The massacre was taken up by agents of social control, the police and coroner, and by various government representatives, and articulated to their respective jurisdictions.

The police were the first on the scene at the Polytechnique, and necessarily responded to the carnage as a policing matter. They secured the area, identified bodies, mapped the killings, and interviewed hundreds of people who were related in any way to the killer: teachers, relatives, friends, gun store employees, and the like, gathering information about Lépine and about possible links between him and his victims. Thirty investigators, working full time with psychologists, psychiatrists, and forensic experts, focused on reconstructing the killer's last days.[78] The coroner's investigation was closely co-ordinated with that of the police. Five days after the massacre, the chief coroner announced that a public inquiry was unlikely: "most of the questions arising from the massacre will be answered by police reports." "Public inquiries are held if the public is not well enough informed about a case," the coroner explained. "In this case the public is very well informed about it."[79] The coroner's office, as Smith writes, "is a state agency. It has a definite legal mandate. It is integral to the state system of control over the use of physical violence by its citizens.... The requirement that the set of descriptive categories be exhaustive with respect to the deaths of which account must be made is a requirement of the state to ensure that every death within the jurisdiction of a given national entity be sanctioned. The set of categories [and] the development of methods of filling categories arise in and as a part of an operation of the state and professional extensions of state interest."[80] The various agencies of social control have institutionalized procedures for assembling, processing and testing information.[81] "What actually happened" has to be produced as a formal record. It is investigated. The resulting account represents the selection, assembly and ordering of the particulars.[82] "The accountability procedures of institutions make some things visible, while others ... do not come into view at all.[83]

Ideological practices are "identified in part with methods of creating accounts of the world that treat it selectively in terms of a predetermined conceptual framework."[84] "They provide analytic procedures for those settings that attend selectively ... thus making only selective aspects of them visible within the institutional order."[85] Issues and questions "that do not fit the framework ... simply do not get entry to the process."[86] It may well be that most of the questions arising from the massacre—those that were allowed entry into the process—were indeed answered by police reports. The police answered questions about weapons, wounds, and the killer's studies, disappointments, and obsessions.[87] Questions they refused to answer were part of the same schema: the content of the suicide letter, what was learned from Lépine's mother and friends, what an examination of his apartment revealed. This refusal left "lots of loose ends," according to a report in the *Globe and Mail*.[88] None of these "ends" is outside the intended schema.

The one-hundred-and-thirty-page coroner's report issued in May of 1990 was similarly circumscribed. Details of the rampage were featured, and more than fifty questions about the emergency response to the massacre asked. The question of a public inquiry was still open at this point. If held, such inquiry would look for answers to the questions posed in the report.[89] Police and coroners' reports are articulated to the function of their respective offices. Questions can be asked about the accuracy and reliability of the statements contained therein, but not about misogyny, not about a backlash against feminism, not about the culture of engineering. Nor do we expect that such questions be asked. "Questions and experiences that do not fit the framework ... do not become part of the textual realities governing decision-making processes."[90] The framework shapes and constrains the way change is envisioned. Accounts do more than define or describe "what happened;" they structure the way one responds. They organize "what happened" in specific ways and provide for a response to what has been identified.[91]

An inquiry was ordered by Public Security Minister Sam Elkas into Quebec emergency services. The responses of police, ambulance services, hospitals, and university security were analyzed. The four-hundred-page report issued by a task force warned that emergency response teams are still "woefully unprepared to deal with a massacre like the one that occurred at Ecole Polytechnique, raising the chilling prospect that random acts of violence could lead to more senseless deaths."[92] One hundred and forty recommendations for improvements to emergency services were made. Having identified the problem as the slow and improvised response of emergency services, the solution provided was the improvement of existing institutions. The possibility that the problem was "the structural issue of power and dependence which render all women and children vulnerable not only to men but to society at large, which is not organized with their interests at heart"[93] was not and could not be entertained.

Government responses were more varied, but no less circumscribed. In anticipation of the second anniversary of the massacre, the *Globe and Mail* itemized government initiatives: December 6 had been declared a national day of commemoration, a bill to control the ownership of guns had been introduced and parliamentary committees had examined the issue of violence against women. Ottawa had set up a national panel to gather and examine evidence on the issue of violence against women and would finance three university centres devoted to research on the matter. "Many women take the government's quick action on this issue to be a signal that it is getting tough on the broader social problem of violence against women," stated the article.[94] What is not apparent in such a listing is the negotiated character of these responses and the manner in which they served to contain the issue of violence within constrained, and constraining, limits.

A call for increased gun control began within hours of the murders. This was no new call, but rather gave new and added voice to an ongoing concern. As reported in *Maclean's*: "Gun laws are almost as old as Canada itself. Legislators first provided penalties for those who carried handguns without a reasonable need for self-defense in 1877. In 1934, Parliament required all handguns to be registered. And in 1977, federal lawmakers moved to control the acquisition of firearms, ban fully automatic weapons outright and establish specific penalties for the use of firearms in criminal acts.... Renewed outcries for tougher legislation followed an incident on Dec. 6, 1989."[95] The murders were "entered" into the legislative terrain, a world of lobbying, briefs, timetables, committees, petitions, presentations, and proposals. Justice Minister Kim Campbell was forced to abandon the first attempt at controls in the fall of 1990 under pressure from western Conservatives.[96] After another round of lobbying, committees and proposals, Bill C-17 received royal assent, two years after the murders. An article in the *Toronto Star* which called the new law a "tribute" to the victims laid out the guidelines: "The new law will restrict firepower, prohibit the import of fully automatic weapons that have been converted to semi-automatic,... and restrict the sale of firearms to people 18 and over.... The new law will ban the 30-round clips Lépine used but not necessarily the rifle."[97] Was this a tribute to the victims or a tribute to compromise? The justice minister negotiated "a polarized debate between those who [wanted] the widest possible ban on guns and those firmly opposed to further controls. Noted Campbell: 'I have two totally different outlooks in my caucus. And I have no intention of tearing our caucus apart.'"[98] The bill passed due to successful negotiation, "a political compromise between competing interests."[99] It did not represent a review and revision of extant social structures and relations.

Francine Pelletier, one of the women targeted by Lépine in his suicide letter, stated in a radio interview that she supported efforts to change the gun laws because it gave Canadians something to organize around, to begin talking about the kind of society we want.[100] This did not happen, at least not in the way one might imagine. One might have imagined the families of those women slain to have been offered some voice in the discussion. Not so. "Families of the victims of the massacre ... [were] told they would not be allowed to address a parliamentary committee studying gun-control legislation because MPs [were] too busy.... The feeling of the majority of the committee was that [they] would get an emotional response from this group, not practical suggestions."[101] There is a particular understanding of rationality that underlies these exclusions. Objectivity and rationality are associated with appearing dispassionate. "Practical suggestions" and negotiated compromises take precedence over real people and how we might feel about them. Facts, "hard facts," "displace and subordinate the actual experience and lives of actual people."[102] Eventually, after intense lobbying by the families of the victims and others, families were allowed to address the committee studying legislation.

Bill C-17 was followed in 1995 by Bill C-68, which improved screening of applicants for gun licences and banned various gun models, including semi-automatic military weapons. It also required the licensing of gun owners and the registration of all firearms by January 1, 2003. The majority of Canadians favour gun control and registration of firearms, but many gun owners are vehemently opposed to these laws and refuse to comply. The law is currently under threat because of cost overruns (estimates of the cost of implementation have risen from two million dollars to one billion), active resistance to it by individual gun owners and interest groups, and "court challenges by several provinces based on the argument that the registry constitutes an encroachment upon provincial property rights."[103] In the run-up to the federal election of January 2006, Stephen Harper vowed to shut down the gun registry, and in June 2006 his Conservative government began the process by tabling legislation to abolish long-gun registry.

The negotiated character of efforts to make legislative changes and the sheer amount of energy and resources required to make even relatively minor changes are clear in Heidi Rathjen's *December 6: From the Montreal Massacre to Gun Control: The Inside Story.* Rathjen, a student at Ecole Polytechnique and at the school on December 6, relates her experience of advocating for gun control, first as a student and then as a representative of the Coalition for Gun Control—the petitions, lobbying, letter-writing campaigns, public meetings, news conferences, parliamentary hearings, and press releases. The arduous work of organizing the campaign was made more difficult by concerted opposition, including threats, from gun owners and lobbies. An enormous expenditure of time, money, and organizational skill resulted only in the modification of existing legislation. The framework of gun control is a narrow one, restricting the terms of the debate (to rights, access, and social control) and possible solutions (to legislative, not social, change). Within the given framework, legislative changes *are* a victory, but not "a wonderful tribute to those fourteen women."

The other major government initiative involved setting up committees and panels to study the issue of violence against women. An all-party subcommittee composed of five female members of parliament was commissioned to undertake the study. Their report, entitled "The War against Women," made twenty-five recommendations, including gender-sensitivity training for judges, law enforcement officers, and members of parliament, the elimination of systemic barriers which prevent women's "equality of opportunity and security," long-term funding for front-line agencies, a housing policy that would make affordable accommodation available, and the establishment of a royal commission on violence. The definition of violence that informed the Committee's thinking was wide ranging: "Violence against women is a multifaceted problem which encompasses physical, psychological, and economic violations of women [and] is integrally linked to the social/economic/political structures, values and policies that silence women in our society, support gender-based discrimination, and maintain women's inequality." The definition "leads to the inevitable conclusion that effective solutions to the problem must involve altering the status of women and traditional values that structure gender relations."[104]

The report, tabled in June, 1991, "echoed what women's groups have been saying for the last decade.... But only Recommendation 25, which said that the government should set up a Royal Commission or panel on violence against women (i.e. study the issue some more) was taken seriously."[105] It "failed to receive endorsement from some Progressive Conservative members of the health and welfare committee because they said parts of it were too feminist and they disliked what they said was a confrontational title."[106] The government's response to the report "The War Against Women" was called "Living Without Fear ... Every Woman's Right, Everyone's Goal." Even the title is an act of containment. The issue is made inclusive (we're all in this together), and refers not to violence but to fear, not to blood and bones and cuts but to a state of mind.

In August, 1991, the federal government established the Canadian Panel on Violence Against Women. The panel heard thousands of testimonies and received hundreds of submissions, all of which made the link between inequality and vulnerability to violence. The document produced from these consultations, entitled "Changing the Landscape: Ending Violence, Achieving Equality (1993)," is comprehensive; the action plan proposed addresses problems in and suggests changes to the Canadian Charter of Rights, the legal system, political and public service sectors, the economy, the family, the tax transfer system, and a variety of other sectors. "Changing the Landscape" is also often moving insofar as it integrates excerpts from many personal accounts of experiences of violence. While emotionally moving, it does not itself provoke movement. This is one of many, even hundreds, of government studies on violence against women, according to the Canadian Research Institute for the Advancement of Women (CRIAW). "Government has taken no action on the majority of the recommendations in these hundreds of reports, particularly in the areas of economic equality and housing which are fundamental necessities for women escaping abuse."[107]

In a commentary on the panel, Marie-Claire Lévesque describes the range of policy responses available to address violence against women. Lévesque refers here specifically to policy on wife assault, but her description can be extended to include policy on other manifestations of violence against women. There are

> four general sets of strategies: research and discussion; education; assistance to survivors and batterers; and restructuring the social system. The preferred government strategies ... are research/discussion (i.e. setting up a committee and examining the issue further) and education (i.e. increasing awareness).... Restructuring society to eliminate the condi-

tions under which violence against women is allowed to occur is not a strategy pursued by the federal government. When it engages in economic restructuring, there is a negative impact on battered women.[108]

Such negative impact was felt a few weeks after the massacre, when core financing to eighty women's groups was eliminated. Despite promises, programs to combat violence were slashed by 1.6 million dollars.[109] Finance minister Michael Wilson claimed that it was "absolutely outrageous" to mention these funding cuts in connection with the murders.[110] This was not simply a conceptual problem, a lack of understanding. It is, rather, a reflection and consequence of institutional organization. "Institutionally differentiated spheres of … control manage the local situations that people experience as a totality."[111] Violence comes under one jurisdiction, budgetary decisions another. Structurally, funding cuts *were* unrelated to the murders, and Wilson was correct in his assertion. After protest, funding was restored, but this was by no means an admission that the massacre and funding cuts that adversely affected women were in some way related. Much less did it initiate a review of government structures and priorities. The restoration of funding was made according to the same terms and within the same framework as the original cuts. The framework itself remained unchanged.

The Canadian government has used the anniversary of the Montreal murders to announce a series of declarations and reports. In 1998 it was the "Iqaluit Declaration of the Federal-Provincial/Territorial Status of Women Ministers on Violence against Women." The declaration is underpinned "by three key strategies: a focus on public education and awareness to change attitudes and behaviour; accessible and responsive services to victims, with a view to preventing revictimization; and effective justice programs to hold perpetrators accountable and provide treatment programs for abusive men."[112] These are all individualized solutions. In December 2002, a news release issued by the Status of Women Canada announced a government report called "Assessing Violence against Women: A Statistical Profile." It acknowledged that "thirteen years after the tragic deaths of 14 young women in Montreal, violence against women in Canada continues to be a persistent social and economic problem." The foreword to the document states: "One of the most informative lessons learned from the attempt to develop these indicators [proxy measures of violence against women] was the need for more data—data that could provide a more complete portrait of women's experiences of violence."[113]

It is clear that the preferred response to violence against women is more study, not "restructuring society to eliminate the conditions under which violence against women is allowed to occur." The United Nations Committee on the Elimination of Discrimination against Women noted the inadequacy of this response, and its 2003 report is critical of Canada's lack of progress in ensuring women's equality on a number of fronts, "including parental leave, childcare and pay equity." It points to high poverty rates and cuts to social services, making a number of recommendations, including sufficient legal aid for women, increased funding for shelters, increased numbers of women in political office, pay equity, and affordable childcare.[114]

The federal government's action on the issue of violence against women is constrained in part by its working definition of "violence." As Gillian Walker explains, violence has become a technical category for non-sanctioned acts beyond bounds of law; it has come to exclude the state's actions.[115] "Male violence" makes gender and power relations visible, but obscures any understanding of society as structured and built on fundamental inequalities that render it disastrously out of tune with human need.[116] Without this understanding, education and awareness are seen as solutions: as Minister Mary Collins claimed, changing men's attitudes is the major challenge.[117]

It is true that the government has taken *some* action on the issue of violence against women, but it is action which contains it as "an issue" ("an important topic of discussion," according to the *Concise Oxford Dictionary*), and fails to recognize it as an indicator of the need for fundamental social transformation. What Ailbhe Smyth writes about men's violence against women in Ireland is equally applicable to the Canadian context: "The State's responses are based on strategies of *containment*. Where a problem is acknowledged, the State (or more correctly, its agents) must now be seen to take action, while at the same time the resolution of the problem must be contained within a framework which ensures that existing power structures, and the interests of the powerful, are not seriously eroded."[118] According to Smith, "institutional structures are set up to organize and control and they do it well."[119] Problems become "specific, contained, cut off from [their] general relation to the whole question of women's oppression in contemporary capitalist society."[120] Structural problems are individualized and personalized, and political questions depoliticized.[121] Education and services to individuals are offered as solutions, and the fundamental structuring of women's oppression remains unchallenged.

The Tenth Anniversary and Beyond

Intransigence to change was *not* the dominant theme in commentaries and at events commemorating the tenth anniversary of the Montreal Massacre. Rather, it focused largely on the many and variety of changes the massacre had wrought. For Michael Kaufman, one of the organizers of the White Ribbon Campaign established in 1991 to enlist men in the campaign to end men's violence against women, "the massacre changed everything." "How often in our lives—not our individual lives, but our collective life—can we identify the exact moment when everything changed for us all?" wrote Kaufman for the tenth anniversary. "For Canadians, there was such a moment.... It was the death of fourteen women.... It was a tragedy that unleashed legislative change, research, new attitudes, and national soul searching that continues to this day."[122]

There were many such lists. Judy Rebick, former head of the National Action Committee on the Status of Women, laid out the impact of the massacre: a dramatic increase in awareness and discussion about violence against women; changes to gun control legislation; strengthening of rape laws; government-sponsored hearings on violence against women; the naming of December 6 as a day of commemoration and action against violence; increased numbers of women in engineering; improvements to safety for women on university campuses; yearly vigils and the establishment of permanent memorials across Canada; the White Ribbon Campaign and the December 6 fund that provides loans to women fleeing violence; and the participation of some unions and corporations in raising awareness of the extent of violence and supporting initiatives that work for change. "Nonetheless," she notes, "like other countries, Canada is a long way from ending the scourge of violence against women and children. In 1998, 185 women were murdered and they were five times more likely to be killed by a spouse than a stranger."[123]

The tenth anniversary was taken up as an opportunity to revisit the massacre, remember and reflect. CBC Newsworld devoted its programming to this effort, broadcasting interviews with relatives of some of the victims, live coverage of several memorial services, presentations on workplace violence, female enrollment in engineering schools, policing practices, changes in male–female relationships, and gun control. The *Globe and Mail*, the *Toronto Star*, and the *Gazette* in Montreal each had extensive coverage. In comparison to articles that appeared shortly after the massacre, there was now more widespread, but by no means universal, consensus that the Montreal Massacre was evidence of inequities between men and women in Canadian society and reflected the consequences of such inequities. In contrast, witness the *Globe and Mail* editorial: "We try to make sense of it by linking it to violence against women. Inevitably, though, it can't be explained as part of a larger social pathology. After 10 years the massacre remains what it was in the beginning: a heinous crime by an isolated gunman."[124]

Anniversary events across the country took a variety of forms, and the Canadian government used its resources to publicize upcoming events. That governmental responses tend to be based on "strategies of containment," as noted above, was reflected in a Web page sponsored by the government of British Columbia offering to announce on its site events commemorating the anniversary. Information requested included the obvious: identification of the sponsoring organization, date, time, location, and so forth. Under "type of event," the copy reads: "Please select from AGM, Art Show, Art Show and Auction, Auction, Awards, Breakfast, Ceremony, Conference, Course, Dinner, Exchange Program, Exhibition, Fair, Forum, Getaway, Lunch, March, Run/Walk, Seminar, Seminar & AGM, Symposium, Tea, Tele-conference, Trade Show, Workshop."[125] Why *these* categories? No room here for acts of civil disobedience, for political protest, for agitating for social change, for anything that might interrupt the decorum of the day.

The overall tone was sombre and congratulatory. This is not surprising. "First mourn, then work for change" has been the banner call for years now. In the mainstream media there were acknowledgements that women continued to be abused and murdered, but highlighted were the changes implemented as a result of murders on December 6. Descriptions of vigils and memorials for the women loomed large, often accompanied by an image of a photogenic woman in mourning, candle or rose in hand. The inauguration of a public monument in Montreal was a frequent point of reference. The fifteenth anniversary was similarly covered in the mainstream press. It was a more sedate anniversary, given that memory of the event fades as the years progress; at universities, where many commemorative events are conducted, entering students were three or four years of age in 1989—December 6 is not a memorable date. Numerous articles on December 7, 2004 minimally reviewed the sequence of events at Ecole Polytechnique in 1989, and then turned to the minute of silence and flags at half-staff on Parliament Hill, the roses laid and candles lit for the women who died, and the speeches from members of parliament about the need for increased law enforcement, for media campaigns to fight violence against women, and for increased funding for shelters.[126] Politicians, Prime Minister Paul Martin among them, spoke of the need to end violence against women. This has been said before, and will be said again.

The Montreal Massacre *has* been a catalyst for change. It "has had the effect of galvanizing politicians, labour groups, institutions and many individual women and men into a determination to catalogue and fight violence against women,"[127] and every anniversary provides the opportunity to raise the issue of gendered violence once again. Although important, a changed interpretation of the massacre and an increased awareness of the violence to which women are subject do not necessarily constitute *real* (that is: "actually existing as a thing or occurring in fact; rightly so called") change.[128] While the extent of violence is increasingly recognized, the material basis for relief is denied, that is, the material basis for independence, equality, and full membership in all social institutions.[129] Just as we have "a public discourse that is impatient with women's fight for equality, because women *have long been declared equal*,"[130] we are fast moving toward a public discourse impatient with the issue of violence because it has long been recognized a problem, and yet the violence continues unabated. A fact sheet on violence against women and girls prepared by the CRIAW reports that half of Canadian women have survived at least one incident of sexual or physical violence; over a quarter (29 per cent) of Canadian women have been assaulted by a spouse; in 1998, 67 women were killed by a current or ex-spouse, boyfriend, or ex-boyfriend. A sidebar on the report notes this: "Governments may talk about equality, but their housing, income, employment, education, criminal justice, immigration, health, home care and child care policies help keep women trapped in abusive relationships. Governments could become a part of the solution, but at this time, they are actively and lethally perpetuating the problem."[131] *Actively and lethally.*

The massacre in Montreal sheds light on violence against women in a way that little else can parallel. It reveals in a particularly horrifying and public way the active repression to which women are subject. It also reveals traces of the "steady institutional process, [which is] equally effective and much less visible in its exclusionary force."[132] "We can see that other forces

[are] at work, more conventional, seemingly more rational, but no less powerful and effective in ensuring the silence of women."[133]

Examining the way the mainstream media and other regulatory institutions presented and processed the massacre makes observable some of those "other forces." Among them are the marginalization of certain voices, the containment of issues within constrained and constraining limits, the representation of feminists as disruptive women who cause the problems they analyze, the individualization and bureaucratization of social problems, and the mystifying distinctions between expert knowledge and ordinary experience. This examination makes observable the *process* of the production of meaning. Meaning is constructed, negotiated, struggled over, and is more than merely conceptual. The framing of "the problem" shapes the response; it is pivotal for determining the appropriate course of action, or lack of same.

Looking for and at the actual practical organization of the production of images, ideas, and concepts given as means for us to think about our world[134] allows us to specify as practices and relations that which is otherwise perceived amorphously as culture or ideology.[135] Such specification is strategically important. The forces constraining us are findable, describable, locatable; they must be identified to be countered. "Power cannot exist apart from actual individuals organizing and working concertedly,… hence the actual power oppressing us is an actual organization of the work and energies of actual people."[136] If this is the case, that oppression is a result of the work and energies of actual people, then the work and energies of actual people can also effectively counter oppression.

These are not the only things that could be said about the relations of power which impinge upon our lives, but they are important things. The terms in which the massacre was discussed are recurring, the silencing ongoing. Today, as two years ago, as five years ago, as twenty-five years ago, female students on university campuses are harassed and targeted, women are killed, guns can be purchased. And the work of processing, reporting on, theorizing about, and managing both victim and violator continues. If we do not examine and explicate the boundaries set by the institutions organizing and regulating society, their invisible determinations will continue to confine us.[137]

3: The Stubborn Particulars of Grace

The Stubborn Particulars of Grace is an attempt to talk about spiritual matters in a political context and to say that if we're going to live in a state of grace, if we're going to live with wholeness or integrity in the world, we have to pay attention to the particulars and politics of where we are. You can't be the transcendent God who saves the world by getting out of it.[1]
— Bronwen Wallace

Grace? How so? The term is often used to refer to those moments when one is immersed in awe at the wondrous beauty that life is. There has been nothing thus far in this discussion of the Montreal Massacre to elicit such a response, nor will there be. However, both Gregory Baum and Bronwen Wallace, whose book of poetry provides the title for this chapter, use the term differently. For Baum, grace can be "experienced as compassion and empowerment, the power to see society as it is and to resist its evil structures."[2] For Wallace there is an implicit imperative: "To live in a state of grace ... pay attention to the particulars and politics of where we are." The backdrop is one of faith and hope, and again, familiar terms are used in an unfamiliar way. With Baum I claim that faith is "the radical inability to accept a people devouring world,"and hope resides in knowing that "the world is meant to be different and ... can be changed."[3]

In order to effect necessary change, we need accounts of the world that originate in some place, from some body—practical accounts of *particular* realities. "There are no universal conditions to be found, only different groups of individuals in concrete contexts for whom emancipation has

particular meanings."[4] Theology has too often fled particularities for gen-
eralities and abstractions in its elaboration of great themes: the nature of
the divine, human nature, love, sin, redemption. The weight of tradition
typically precludes attention to painful realities in the local and immediate. But a flight into generality and abstraction leaves those painful realities unchallenged. Here, I follow the imperative to attend to actual lives,
actual people, and the concrete situations in which we find ourselves. In
doing so I stand with other feminist liberationists who begin there also.
Carter Heyward, for instance, writes that she is "learning the critical necessity of approaching our theological work ... through the particularities of
our lives-in-relation."[5] Such an approach to theological work does not
mean a confinement to details or the isolation of one particularity from
another, one act of violence from another. Particularity is not myopic. It
does not preclude the recognition of patterns and the making of connections; it requires them.

In order to take up the December 6 massacre and responses to it and
enter them into a more explicitly theological forum, theologically naming the issues raised and articulating theological implications, I rely again
on Gregory Baum, who suggests categories and models possibilities. Three
of his claims concerning practical theology are used as points of departure:
that there must be dialogue between theology and the social sciences in
order that social evil might be understood and conversion from ideological distortion possible,[6] that it is necessary to heed the voices that interrupt the dominant discourse,[7] and that the theologian must decide whether
to join the dominant discourse or turn to a counter discourse.[8] Following
Baum, who uses sociological categories and conclusions to put flesh and
bones on theology,[9] the analysis developed in the previous chapter is
brought forward to name distortions, to heed interruptions, and to describe
the choice that must be made.

Naming

In the opinion of Mordecai Richler, the massacre was "the act of an
absolutely demented man [which does not] lend itself to any explanation."[10] "It would not surprise me if one of the demons that tortured Marc
Lépine was the steady torrent of abuse directed at men in general by too
many feminists," wrote F.M. Christensen, a professor at the University of
Alberta.[11] According to Elaine Audet, "fourteen women, young, intelligent,

full of dreams ... were coldly gunned down with the premeditation of three thousand years of woman-hating, reinforced by patriarchal societies built upon the domination of women and their children."[12] A "litany of social ills created Marc Lépine," wrote columnist Michael Valpy. "The stone weights of poverty and powerlessness on families. The urban isolation. The depersonalized workplace. The ghastly cultural images of resolution ... get your gun, get your military fatigues, be a man."[13]

As varied as these comments are, they each attempt to explain the evil, to name its source. At one end of the belief spectrum is the personalization of sin. Its locus is the individual psyche, both in genesis and culpability. The impact of social structures and cultural hegemony on individuals is not considered. At the other end, all of society is to blame. The deterioration of the entire social fabric is responsible for the manifestation of evil. Here, misogyny is lost in a sea of social ills, and the problem relativized. "A too quick turn to universals ... blinds us to the insidious and pervasive manifestations of this particular form of oppression.... The words may be true, but when used to avoid confronting the specific problems of sexism they are radically untruthful."[14] And in the middle? Blaming feminists ignores three thousand years of woman hating. The concept of "three thousand years of woman hating" ignores the specific forms that domination has taken and the equally long history of women's resistance. Such a position "generalizes and abstracts the event in ways that divert our attention from the particular circumstances and context.... Lack of acknowledgment of the specific context and target of this horrifying act allows us to deplore it as violence but does not provide any way of holding accountable the activities of the state and the media over the years in trivializing, marginalizing, and increasingly (to use Michele Landsberg's term) 'demonizing' feminism.'"[15]

None of these positions condones the violence of December 6. The act was universally abhorred. But it is not sufficient simply to recognize sin, if that implies condemnation without analysis. Failure to attend to the concrete conditions that deny justice can result in fixing blame at random. If strategies for change are to be developed and transformation to be made possible, it is necessary to specify, "to render determinate, in the analysis ... of specific situations and circumstances, specific dimensions of human sinfulness, individual and social."[16]

What has been specified here? Clearly and unequivocally, the murder of fourteen women was an act of evil. But this ultimate act of suppression was followed by other acts of suppression which ensured silence in more conventional ways. An identification of those other acts is an identification of ideological distortions. Dorothy Smith's description of ideological practices directs my analysis: "Ideological practices are pervasive features of the organization of the disjuncture between the relations of ruling and the actualities of people's lives they organize and govern.... [They] ensure that the determinations of our everyday, experienced world remain mysterious by preventing us from making them problems for inquiry."[17] Ideology identifies *"the interested procedures which people use as a means not to know."*[18] This understanding allows us to identify several distortions.

'The vast orchestration and channelling of interpretations into nonthreatening territories'

"More than at any other time in my life, I felt the seemingly inexorable weight of this patriarchal society's safety mechanisms," wrote Margot Lacroix, reflecting on her reaction to the murders at Ecole Polytechnique. They were devastating in themselves, and equally disturbing was "the vast orchestration and channelling of interpretations into nonthreatening territories."[19] There were a number of means by which this was accomplished, among them admonitions to silence, the dispersal of the murders through regulatory institutions, pathologization of the murderer, reliance on professional expertise for explanatory purposes, recourse to the myth of a coherent society, and the privileging of mourning as the acceptable response to murderous violence.

Admonitions to silence In the immediate aftermath of the murders, vigils and marches were held across the country. A letter to the editor of *Le Devoir* from a participant at a march in Montreal described efforts by male student leaders to prevent women from speaking to the crowd, insisting that this was a time for silence and prayer.[20] This was not an isolated incident. Many women who spoke publicly about the context in which the murders took place were reprimanded for acting inappropriately; as politicians such as Jacques Parizeau, the leader of the Parti Québécois, and many others insisted, silence was the only way to commemorate this tragedy.[21] In anticipation of the fifth anniversary, members of the student association at Ecole Polytechnique shared their views with other student associations on an appropriate method to remember the day, favouring silence and white ribbons and opposing "big signs" and "loud speeches." "We prefer to dedicate this day to personal reflection, from which positive actions generally come out, instead of acting loudly for peace."[22] Silence out of respect for the dead is a time-honoured response, but when imposed it shows not respect for the dead but disdain for the living. Silence imposed is censorship, and in this case indicative of a widespread reluctance to directly address the issue of men's violence against women. Silence in the face of it allows its perpetuation.

Dispersal The massacre, as an event requiring action, was dispersed over several institutional sites and accommodated to the purview of each site. The various accommodations generated a proliferation of related but distinct analyses of "the problem" and ways to solve it—analyses and solutions restricted to and regulated by the conceptual framework and work practices of the particular office. Issues are depoliticized as they are channelled through regulatory institutions. The proliferation and channelling of both analysis and response restrict the possibility of a collective construction of issues and problems. The gun-control movement is a case in point. Once the murders were entered into the arena of legislation and regulation, the fact that it was *women* who were shot by a self-identified feminist hater became a peripheral issue, at best. Access to guns and rights to gun ownership continue to be hotly contested, not so the numbers of women killed with guns and many other weapons.

Pathology One of the sites to which the massacre was dispersed was the psychiatric. Dorothy Smith writes that psychiatry can give us ways of analyzing an act that prevent us from recognizing or opposing directly the situation in which that act arises.[23] The pathologization of the killer individualized his act, locating the problem in his (unique) psyche and his (personal) social history, and gave rise to questions such as this: "The world is full of little boys who are brutally abused and consistently disappointed and who do not grow up into killers.... So, the hard question is: why does one particular person every now and then cross the line from fantasy to reality?"[24] And this: "How is it possible to have in the same person the coexistence of seemingly normal behaviour and, at the same time, the will and the capacity to plan meticulously such a mad and monstrous act?... How could such dangerous persons be detected and positively identified?"[25] Recourse to individual pathology points us toward the problem of identifying individual offenders, not that of social transformation.

Professionalism In the early days especially, a variety of professionals were called upon to discuss the murders, criminologists, psychologists, and other experts. Although it is natural to turn for insight to people trained to deliver objective, rational analysis, Smith raises questions about professional norms that value intellectual consistency and coolness, impersonality, detachment, and objectivity.[26] Professional knowledge separates expertise from outrage. Taking a position in the hierarchical structure of the professions often means separating oneself from those whose partial and "emotional" involvement prevents "detached" and "logical" discussion of the problem, notes Smith.[27]

The professionals called upon to comment on the massacre have been precisely that—professional—giving the impression of detachment and objectivity required for one considered deserving of the designation. At what cost, one wonders. There is a self-regulating dimension to this "channelling of interpretations into nonthreatening territories." Rational analysis is held as distinct from, and valued above, unbridled emotion. Feminist theologian Beverly Harrison challenges such distinctions. Anger is "a sign of some resistance in ourselves to the moral quality of the social relations in which we are immersed. Extreme and intense anger signals a deep reaction to the action upon us or toward others to whom we are related."[28] Emotion tends to action.[29] If anger is an appropriate, a mobilizing, a life-giving response, absolute distinctions between emotional responses and considered solutions are inappropriate, demobilizing, and death dealing.

The myth of a coherent society The channelling of the massacre through institutional and professional frames restricts what is visible, what can be thought and acted upon.[30] Vision is further impaired by the glossing over of horror, a quick turn from the face of violence. The emphasis on our collective shock and our shared grief in the immediate aftermath of the massacre made it possible to cling to the myth of a coherent society. We could even feel good about ourselves: "I'm glad to say I feel a little better now than I did just after the tragedy," wrote Josh Freed, a journalist for the Montreal *Gazette*. "The response to it has been remarkably sincere and civilized and has restored some of my faith in our city.... Montreal's reaction has lifted my spirits."[31] The myth of a coherent society is not simply a refuge in troubled times; it was actively reproduced. Recall the admonishments to silence, the turn to tears, not anger, and the many efforts to minimize the significance of the gender of the victims: not a crime against women, but against humanity. Not "The War against Women," but "Living without Fear ... Everyone's Goal."[32] "We're all in this together."

Privileging of mourning If interpretations of the murders have been channelled into nonthreatening territories, so to have memorializing responses to it. Routinely every year, major papers report on a vigil or memorial service commemorating December 6, often accompanied by a photograph of a woman in mourning, bathed in candle light, or a well-known public figure with a rose in hand. What are we to make of this? That such is the appropriate and acceptable response? It would appear that acceptable responses are relatively passive ones; in this case, the discreetly emotional mourning of the dead. In a number of articles, Sharon Rosenberg raises questions around the fact that "vigils are being implicitly encouraged as preferred acts of remembrance."[33] To the degree that vigils encourage us to reflect back rather than move forward, they too are acts of containment.

Trivialization by equalization

A variant of channelling interpretations into non-threatening territories is to channel them into supposedly threatened territories, in this case, the territory of male privilege. Defence of that privilege took several forms, one of which was the equating of the massacre with vigils at which men were asked to step back or stay away. For example, one person commented: "Has it not sunk in yet that separating the men from the women is precisely what Marc Lépine did? To ask men and women to separate at a public ceremony ... is to reinforce, rather than deny, the gender divisions expressed by Lépine's extreme act of violent sexism."[34] This type of hermeneutic turns from the face of violence not so much by hurrying elsewhere but by levelling it out.

Dorothy Smith maintains that ideological thinking "confines us to a conceptual level divorced from its ground,"[35] and separate concepts from their necessary anchorage in the world. It is only by divorcing these quite different separations from their respective contexts and histories that such comparisons can become possible and even persuasive. "Ideology deprives us of access to, hence of critique of, the social relational substructure of our experience."[36] "The different locations, activities, and implications are lost."[37] If the different locations, activities and implications are restored, it is *not* the same thing for Lépine to have separated men from women, and for some women to have organized "women-only" vigils. One separation was for murderous intent; the other to provide a safe space for women to mourn; one involved no choice, the other, much—men who wished to participate in vigils had several options open to them. To equate these two separations, and to suggest that the latter *reinforces* the former, is a gross misrepresentation.

A variant of this particular ideological practice is found in the frequently heard objection that feminist commentary on the murders depicted all men as complicit to some extent, if not murderous brutes. An editorial by George Bain in *Maclean's* shortly after the second anniversary (and quoted again in *Maclean's* just prior to the tenth) commented on media coverage of anniversary events and carried the headline "An orgy over whether all men are vile."[38] On the twelfth anniversary, the headline of an article describing efforts to promote the White Ribbon campaign in a student newspaper at the University of Western Ontario read, quite inexplicably, "Men are evil." Many women found themselves in the position of having to reassure their male partners or colleagues that *they* were good and honourable men, unlike the murderer in any way. This conflation of categories (that one mass murderer was the same as every man who has abused a woman was the same as every man) is a fictional construct that serves to deflect attention from the actual content of women's political analyses. It shifts the terms of the discussion from calls to confront and oppose all forms of violence done to women by men to reassurances to men of their own individual innocence. Recourse to individual culpability, or lack of same, in this case, points us toward consoling and applauding all the good men out there, leaving calls for social transformation lost in the clamour.

The most sustained airing of the fiction that *all* men were being castigated occurred around proposals for a women's monument in Vancouver, the inscription to read, in part, "In memory, and in grief, for all the women who have been murdered by men." Henry Gale's reflection on his own response to the inscription is to the point:

> I thought I was being blamed, as a man, for what had happened in Montreal. Not all men are murderers, I quickly countered, Why, then, say "murdered by men"?... Two things occurred that changed my mind. The sheer virulence of the attacks on the project by several Vancouver newspaper columnists was disquieting. All male, they cantankerously insisted that the whole thing was a calculated insult to men. By implication, they were suggesting that the women behind the project were exploiting the deaths of those 14 women, as a means of promoting hatred against men.... The world is drowning in a rising tide of brutality. And the grim truth is that the violence is overwhelmingly perpetrated by men. Once, I plucked the "male" from "male violence" out of a misplaced

sense of impartiality. By doing so, I rendered violence a causeless phenomenon, like the weather, which Canadian men and women have to endure. But there is a human face behind the fist, and most of the time, it's a man's. If we keep that face in shadow out of a mistaken sense of propriety, then how will the violence cease?... "Men who are decent, non-violent and law abiding accept the truth of the inscription, realizing the issue is not about collective guilt but collective responsibility."[39]

Distortion of reality continuum

In a talk called "Feminism in the Media and the '90s Backlash," Rose Simone refers to a "distortion of reality continuum" in the context of having collected numerous articles from mainstream news sources with headlines stating that white men are discriminated against, when in fact the upper ranks of corporations and the halls of power are overwhelmingly dominated by white males. "It would make a great Twilight Zone episode," she notes.[40] On a distortion-of-reality continuum the violator can become a victim, and sympathy elicited, and our shock at violence can be regarded as proof that we live in a non-violent society.[41] Oppression can be blamed on those subjected to it, and feminist theorizing can be taken not as a response to violence but the reason for it. According to Simone, there is "such unbalanced presentation that the mainstream media either ignores, or actually skews, warps and misrepresents what serious feminist women are saying and what feminism was about."

Such skewing, warping, and misrepresentation are analyzed in Catherine Nelson-McDermott's "Murderous Fallout: Post-Lépine Rhethoric." The author considers some of the rhetorical strategies that appeared in the *Edmonton Journal* that were used to deny "even the possibility that Marc Lépine's actions might have been an extension of misogynist attitudes that permeate our society." Nelson-McDermott delineates tactics that portray feminists as opportunistic, erase their argument, and carry an implied threat that protesting violence perpetuates it. One strategy was a type of begging the question, refusing arguments that looked to systemic reasons for violence against women, or conflating "misogynist attitudes" with attitudes held by all men. Another "rhetorical tactic common to these responses is a type of *ad feminam* fallacy, an attack on the feminist rather than a discussion of her position, which results in an insidious portrayal of feminists as wildly irrational and opportunistic, somewhat 'mad' or at the very least, 'unnatural.'"[42]

Anti-feminism is the *political response* of men to the *political voice* of women.[43] Rose Marie Kennedy comments on the stakes:

> The political significance of maintaining the feminist meaning of the Montreal massacre runs incredibly deep. Those who would have us believe that the massacre was not about violence against women have a great deal at stake. They want to maintain the myth that the heterosexually organized nuclear family is safe, that women bring their own misfortune upon themselves when we participate more fully in public institutions, and that the source of our pain is individual, and not socially organized and maintained. It's this myth that binds us up, that makes us doubt ourselves, and prevents us from challenging the status quo.[44]

There are a number of other ideological practices to consider. Add the linguistic degendering of violence in terms such as "family violence" or "domestic disturbance." Add the selective memory by which we readily call to mind fourteen young white women, university educated, poised on promising careers, and "forget" the women whose remains have been found at a pig farm in Port Coquitlam, British Columbia. Add these things, and more, and one is left with the image of constructed blindness. Ideological practices prevent us from knowing what we know. They mask relations of domination, disorganize our ability to make connections, and inhibit the possibility of collective action. Such practices can set limits on our theological horizons as well, rendering our work counterproductive to what theology should be about: justice making and empowering for social change. We can look and not see, know much and nothing.

"Ideology ensures the absolute guarantee that everything really is so."[45] Conversion from ideological distortion begins with the recognition that everything is not so. It is a task of practical theology to explode the illusions of mainstream culture that disguise injustice so as to give greater social stability, says Baum.[46] To rupture these illusions is to break the limitations on perception and to create new ways of seeing and knowing.[47]

Interruption

When the dominant public discourse obscures relations of domination, interruption is an important theological category.[48] The analysis pursued here takes up the standpoint of women, a standpoint outside the ruling apparatus and critical of it. It explores the gaps between what women have been given and what we require.[49] Where does *this* direct us? What shall

we do? We must read the gaps and reread what we have been given. Looking upon the world from its underside "introduces an element of rupture
or discontinuity in regard to the world as it is communicated ... by the cultural agents of society," writes Baum.[50] This element of rupture should not
be suppressed but amplified. If we mean to be prophets we must disrupt
the dominant narrative, disclose its distortions, resist its silencing effects,
and say something else, something different.

Interruption begins with a critique of structures that silence and practices that prevent us knowing what we know. It continues with "no." No,
it was not inexplicable. No, it was not an isolated incident. "Women may
be the only 'many' left who are never attacked because of who they are—
the persecution is never deliberate, it is said, never systemic, always just
an isolated incident."[51] "It is important to assert the connections between
[various] episodes of violence because it helps to dispel the powerful,
silencing notion that they are isolated incidents that have nothing to do with
one another, or with the oppression of women."[52] Violence against women
is the most pervasive, least recognized human rights issue.[53]

> If all femicides were recognized as such and accurately counted, if the
> massive incidence of non-lethal sexual assaults against women and girls
> were taken into account, if incest and battery were recognized as torture
> (frequently prolonged over years), if the patriarchal home were seen as
> the inescapable prison it so frequently becomes, if pornography and
> gorenography were recognized as hate literature, then this culture might
> have to acknowledge that we live in the midst of a reign of sexist terror.[54]

Even this is insufficient. A listing of the myriad manifestations of
violence is inadequate if analysis is confined to the domain of "interpersonal relations:" those men doing those things to girls and women. Of
course it is about men and women and the relationships among us, about
identity, sexuality, and socialization. But gender cannot be regarded merely
as the property of individuals. It is also a principle of social organization,
"a system of power, hierarchy and privilege, of imposed inequality."[55]
Reservation of the term "violence" in the phrase "violence against
women" to individual instances of verbal or physical abuse by men
excludes from consideration other acts of violence that are deleterious to
the well-being of women: lack of pay equity, under-representation in
every kind of decision-making body, and the commodification of
women's bodies in the media, for instance. The problem of violence
against women cannot be solved at the level of individuals, one heart at

a time, without any recognition that individual hearts are formed in the crucible of society. The system of power, privilege, and imposed inequality, in all its manifestations, must be held accountable.

Men who act violently toward women are, in effect, acting as agents of a patriarchal structure, helping to ensure its perpetuation. Most individual perpetrators would not understand themselves so, but at least one certainly did. Lépine explicitly stated that he was targeting women who had stepped out of place. Violence is often an effort to control women, or punish those who have escaped the boundaries of control, hence the increased risk of femicide when a woman has left an abusive relationship. Violence as a means of control has impact far beyond the mind and body of the individual woman beaten or murdered. "Feminist researchers and educators have long argued that the fear of violence interferes with and constricts women's full participation in everyday life.... [It] can be understood to serve as a social control function insofar as the impact of the violent actions of some men potentially keeps all women in a state of fear, and results in the self-imposition of restrictions and limits in most women's lives."[56]

In a study of women killed in Ontario between 1974 and 1994, Rosemary Gartner and colleagues note that the killings "reflect important dimensions of gender stratification, such as power differences in intimate relations and the construction of women as sexual objects generally, and as sexual property in particular contexts." As such, intervention strategies to protect women at risk "must be coupled with efforts to address the underlying sources of intimate femicide. If ... the sources lie at least in part in attitudes and behaviours that have been supported for centuries by patriarchal systems of power and privilege, those attitudes and behaviours, as well as the systems supporting them, must be confronted and contested."[57]

Gartner's call to address underlying sources of femicide is, in theological parlance, a call to address social sin. Sin is both personal and social. It is most readily recognizable in individual acts of violence, but by no means limited to such acts. Baum delineates four levels of social sin, each of which was manifest in the Montreal Massacre and responses to it. Social sin can reside in institutions, in ideologies, in the "approving consciousness of people caught in the ideology;" and in collective decisions which exacerbate injustice.[58] First, "*social sin is made up of the injustices and dehumanizing trends built into the various institutions—social, political, economic, religious, and others—which embody people's collective life."*[59] Consider universities. Until relatively recently women were not welcomed into the hallowed halls of academe. Although women have made inroads on many fronts, making up at least half the enrollment in schools of medicine and law, engineering schools lag far behind. Prior to December 1989, female enrollment rates hovered at 13 per cent; a decade later, they had risen to 20 per cent. Monique Frize has written of the barriers facing women who wish to pursue careers in engineering. The culture in engineering schools is masculine; it "stresses the importance of technology over personal relationships, formal abstract knowledge over inexact humanistic knowledge, and male attributes over female ones." There is a "chilly climate" for female faculty and students, and sexist or sexual comments can still be heard.[60] It was no accident that an engineering school was chosen by the murderer on December 6. He considered it the proper domain of males, a view supported by the culture of engineering and institutional practices.

Second, *"social sin is made up of the cultural and religious symbols, operative in the imagination and fostered by society, that legitimate and reinforce the unjust institutions and thus intensify the harm done to a growing number of people."* Consider the funeral mass of nine of the fourteen murdered women at Montreal's Notre Dame Basilica. The mass was presided over by a host of men in religious garb, and media coverage highlighted the dark-suited male political figures in attendance such as the prime minister and the mayor of Montreal. A ritual intended to provide comfort for the living and lay to rest the dead was undercut by an overwhelming preponderance of males in active roles. Men surrounded the altar, delivered the sermon, and led the funeral procession; women, except for those who lay lifeless in white coffins, were relegated to the sidelines. This display of male power and prestige underscored the underlying causes of the very deaths these men intended to commemorate. The role of Christianity in perpetuating the myth of male superiority and the proper spheres of male and female activity cannot be overlooked. The biblical myth depicting woman as second in creation and subordinate to her husband, Paul's injunctions that women should be silent, theological commentary that portrayed women as the devil's gateway (Tertullian) or misbegotten male (Augustine), and centuries during which women were not considered appropriate candidates for ministerial roles have taken their toll.

Third, *"social sin refers to the false consciousness created by these institutions and ideologies."* Consider sexism. The secondary or derivative status of females is so deeply ingrained in institutions, regulatory systems, and individual and collective consciousness that it seems normal and natural that most engineering graduates are male and most nursing graduates female; female engineers are anomalous. Sexism is so deeply ingrained that it can go almost entirely unremarked that only males were solicited to speak on the national news on December 6, 1989.[61]

Fourth, "*social sin is made up of the collective decisions, generated by the distorted consciousness, which increase the injustices in society and intensify the power of the dehumanizing trends.*" Consider government and legal decisions that make budget cuts to women's shelters, like those that occurred within weeks of December 6, 1989, or deny pay equity; in November 2004, the Supreme Court ruled that Newfoundland was justified in deferring a pay-equity increase for health care workers because of financial constraints, even as it acknowledged that "the province contravened the Charter of Rights and Freedoms and made women appear to be second-class citizens."[62] Decisions and policies which deny support and justice for women are reflective of and contribute to women's devaluation.

Sin is both personal and social. In forgetting the social dimension of sin, we lose "the key for understanding the violence in our history and the collective evil in which we are involved."[63] "All things considered, [Marc Lépine] was no young man. He was as old as all the sexist, misogynist proverbs, as old as all the Church fathers who ever doubted women had a soul. He was as old as all the legislators who ever forbade women the university, the right to vote, access to the public sphere."[64]

Choice

The task of practical theology … includes at the very beginning a critical analysis of society's structured injustices. For the theologian must decide whether to join the dominant discourse or … turn to a counter discourse.[65]

Inquiry into the specific forms and process by which the Montreal Massacre came to be presented as it did, and various oppositions to that presentation, illuminate the features of two quite different geographies. One has maps, and "lights to show us/ when to walk, where to turn."[66] It tells us that this society is civilized and compassionate, that acts of violence are individual aberrations, that we will be safe if we do not go out at night.

It is the voice that says to an outraged women: "be calm, be silent." It decries a crime against humanity and laments lost innocence; it prays for acceptance, offers comfort, and hopes for reconciliation. This is familiar territory, well lit, well marked, well policed, and well known. The other geography crosses boundaries; the view is more expansive. Against the seemingly coherent, dominant discourse is a broad range of other, more or less comprehensive, more or less coherent and developed alternative discourses. Here are the voices that say that this act of violence against fourteen women is of a piece with other acts of violence against many more. Here are the cries of outraged women: "enough and too much." Here are those who refuse to accept the unacceptable. This is less familiar territory. The shadows are deeper and the signs unfamiliar; the borders shift and expand. These geographies generate different maps of the world and confront one with a choice: to join the dominant discourse or turn to, and help create, a counter discourse. This choice is neither simple nor arbitrary, but it is fundamentally important. On it depends how we understand and name good and evil, justice and injustice, change and possibility.

The dominant discourse, widely disseminated and readily available, has the weight and force of long-established structures, and many voices, to carry it. Within this discourse it *is* possible to mourn the loss of life, to abhor senseless brutality, to condemn specific kinds of violence against women, to respond to discrete, if many, acts. In responding to discrete, if many, acts, the dominant discourse masks relations of domination; the depth, extent, and pervasive nature of misogynous violence are hidden. As Baum observes, "the cultural mainstream tends to disguise from people social sin and exploitation operative in society."[67] As goes the analysis so too do possibilities for change. The dominant discourse paints a picture of a coherent, civilized society interrupted briefly by unconnected acts of incoherence and incivility. Society is not fundamentally disordered, but some of its members are profoundly so. They must be identified, helped, controlled, their victims counselled, protected, and saved. Poster campaigns, television ads, and tightened gun-control legislation are the major strategies; changing attitudes is the major challenge.

The dominant discourse is dominant, but it is not master. To quote Gillian Walker: "The process by which social reality is constructed results in there being considerable discrepancy and disjunction between the ideological forms provided for us to understand our world and our direct experience of our situation in that world."[68] A counter discourse is generated by those who experience the discrepancy between the forms provided for us to understand our world and our experience of it *as* discrepancy. The discomfort that discrepancy provokes is distressing, at the very least, and is also of value epistemologically. The non-coincidence between what we are given and what we require opens up the possibility of rereading what has been given.[69] The counter discourse articulated by those critical of the characterization of the massacre in the mainstream media and within regulatory institutions is both description and critique. It offers a description of a society fundamentally at odds with the well-being of girls and women, and a critique of existing institutions and social structures. It discloses the inadequacy of the dominant apparatuses of the social system, and claims that they are attained and maintained through exclusion, mystification, and repression.

As understandings of violence must be expanded, so too must reconciliation and healing. Prayers at the funeral mass for nine of the fourteen women at Notre Dame Basilica in Montreal called "for hope and forgiveness on the part of those left behind."[70] But forgiveness and hope are not enough. The Marxian critique, that theology abstracts concrete contradictions, giving symbolic solutions for real problems, stands as a corrective to the Christian tendency to substitute theory for practice, to substitute an account of the transcendence of alienation for its achievement.[71] The imaginative, if hope-filled, leap to reconciliation prescinds from the necessity of making real its possibility. It disguises the real conflicts in the community and the inequality of power.[72] True reconciliation is contingent upon the recognition of evildoing and the redress of injustice. We *do* need to be healed from the ravages of violence. But neither time and forgetfulness nor hope and prayer, by themselves, beget healing. As Andrea Dworkin states, "Fighting back is as close to healing as we are going to come."[73]

Rereading what we have been given means rereading even God. Where is God in the face of such horror? According to the homilist at the funeral mass, Cardinal Paul Grégoire, Archbishop of Montreal, "God is silently present."[74] Cardinal Paul-Emile Léger claimed that "the death of these women must be seen as 'an offering made to God.'"[75] A silent God who receives broken bodies is a God with whom we can share only silence and despair. Alone with the Alone. A different understanding of God links us to others and compels us to action. For Baum, and for me, "God is the abiding pain we experience in the face of a suffering, oppressed and hungry humanity,"[76] offering not comfort and solace, but restlessness and yearning. God summons us to recognize sin, and shakes us free from inherited categories.[77] God's grace "takes the form of an infinite, unquenchable longing for justice."[78]

The theologian must decide whether to join the dominant discourse or turn to a counter discourse, to walk the levelled plain or explore chasms. The criterion on which to decide is not some notion of definitive or abstract truth. Every reading of reality is from some position, and serves some end. This does not mean that each reading is equally valid. There are better and less good readings of reality, better and less good ways of generating readings. They are to be weighed in terms of the comprehensiveness of what is included for analysis, the hope or despair offered in consequence of that analysis, and the response generated, the change required. A better reading illuminates existing social relations rather than masking them. It examines more and assumes less; it makes more visible, more possible, and is more inclusive. The choice to be made *is* a choice between discourses, between opposing ideas, but it is also much more than that. At stake are not simply ideas in opposition, but lives, and death. As such, it is a choice to be made not primarily in terms of the relative merits of discourse but in terms of commitments and consequences, its verification shown in the transformation of individuals and social relations. With whom do we stand?

Naming distortions, asserting connections, and deprivatizing violence, reconciliation, and even God are ways in which the dominant narrative is disrupted. There is yet another kind of interruption, one which proceeds not so much by contradiction as through creation. The approach in this chapter has been largely deconstructive, a critical taking-apart and scrutiny of a variety of responses to the Montreal Massacre, one which focuses primarily on debates over meaning. I turn now to more explicitly reconstructive projects, to a sampling of individual and community responses that engage the debates reflected here, and take them forward.

4: What Shall We Tell Our Bright and Shining Daughters?

"They are so precious to us, our daughters," began Stevie Cameron, writing shortly after the massacre of fourteen women in Montreal. "We tell our bright, shining girls that they can be anything.... But as they grow and learn, with aching hearts we have to start dealing with their bewilderment about injustice.... What can we say to our bright and shining daughters?"[1]

— Stevie Cameron

I remember that night, more clearly than I remember Wednesday night two weeks ago. The news was on in the other room. I heard something indistinct about shootings and stretchers and went to see what had happened. There were women shot, the numbers still mounting, at a university in Montreal.

No, it can't be. Not in this country; not at a university; not so many; not all women. In the days and weeks following, I read everything, listened to everything, and tried to make some sense of it all. Despair and disbelief soon turned to something else, something that welled up and would not be contained. I took pen to paper, and began to write. I write to see, to understand, and in times of trouble, to exorcize the demons that lie within. As Anne Tyler says, "for me, writing something down is the only road out."[2]

That need to do *something,* to respond *somehow,* was widely shared, and took every form conceivable. The massacre sparked a massive response, a channelling of outrage into representation, organization, and action; a reassertion of life in the face of death. Women alone in their rooms sculpted, painted, prayed. Women together organized: new women's groups were formed, films produced, plays staged, symposia on violence organized, and art exhibits mounted. Men too responded, their numbers fewer but their commitment firm. We gathered in memory of fourteen women to share our grief; to symbolize our strength and solidarity; to examine the insidious forms that violence takes.

These many and varied responses are nothing less than acts of *resistance*. Theologian Beverly Wildung Harrison writes that "where there is and has been oppression, there is also, always, a history of survival and resistance to oppression that needs to be recalled and celebrated for the marks of dignity, courage, and potential it bears."[3] An appreciation of the many ways women and men resist oppression is absolutely critical. We are bludgeoned on a daily basis by reports and images of violence enacted against women. The realization that the violence is so widespread, so damaging, and so deadly can lead to paralysis. Keeping in mind the ways we resist, relentlessly and fiercely resist, is necessary to counter despair.

Recurring Elements

While the murders themselves were almost absurdly predictable in the way they were carried out, responses to them were not. On one hand: a gun, army fatigues, and a methodical targeting of women. *That* particular script is readily available, unavoidable in fact. In response: art, music, protest, vigils—creative and diverse acts of defiance. By way of recalling and celebrating such acts, recurring motifs/elements in a sampling of responses to December 6 are sketched below.

Testimony

In the immediate wake of the murders, police advised reporters not to dwell on the fact that all the victims were women because they feared an unstoppable flow of male, anti-feminist violence. However, it was female testimony that refused to be contained.[4] Is there any woman whose life has not been touched by violence in some form or another? The stories began to pour forth, as woman after woman told of her own experience. "Naming the violence ... and sharing that knowledge in any form is, in and of itself, an act of resistance that rarely makes its way into public discourse."[5] A 1999 report from Johns Hopkins University that surveyed violence against women world-wide indicated that "in some countries, almost 70% of abused women surveyed said they had never told anyone about their abuse before being asked in the interview."[6] In a dramatic way, the reality of violence *did* make its way into public discourse after December 6 as stories were told and connections made.

Listening and speaking open into the possibility of relationship, a means out of isolation and into the hearing, the reach, of others. Sharing the intimacies of our lives, in this case the acts that violate them, can release fears and emotions that may well have been festering for years. The virtue of testimony is more than cathartic, however, although it is certainly that. Through the telling of our stories, patterns begin to emerge. *What happens to me happens to others; it is not my pain only.* "Moving from silence into speech is ... a gesture of defiance that heals, that makes new life and new growth possible."[7] Knowledge of each other's lives and experiences can provide a basis for systemic social transformation.[8]

The way in which testifying unfolds and is received is not unambiguous, as Wendy Hui Kyong Chun points out in an article that explores the tensions surrounding the relative lack of testimony from women who were actually at Ecole Polytechnique on December 6 and testimony of others who were not present. "What happens when an event seems to invoke testimony not only from its survivors (who are eerily silent), but also from those who were never physically present, from those who seem to be testifying belatedly to another event?"[9] What happens, according to Chun, are conflicts over *who* has the right to speak and *in what way*. There was a rift "between certain older feminists and younger women—usually women in male-dominated fields—who resented the older feminists' commentary and their imposition and usurpation of 'victim' status."[10]

Chun makes the case for "a politics and practice of listening as a necessary complement to a politics of testifying," so that various testimonies do not compete but rather resonate with one another. "This contract of listening must be accompanied by a politics that understands acts of violence not as 'representative of' or 'substitutable for' each other, but by a politics that sees these acts as forceful because they recall other events, because they open the self to others."[11] Opening the self to others through the telling of our stories opens also the possibility of collective actions for change.

Names/Naming

Geneviève Bergeron, Hélène Colgan, Nathalie Croteau
Barbara Daigneault, Anne-Marie Edward, Maud Haviernick
Barbara Klucznik Widajewicz, Maryse Laganière, Maryse Leclair
Anne-Marie Lemay, Sonia Pelletier, Michèle Richard
Annie St-Arneault, Annie Turcotte

Virtually every vigil, every poster, and every memorial site names the women murdered. Lin Gibson, "aware that the names of victims are quickly forgotten, disappearing into history as empty statistics,"[12] created four artistic memorials naming the fourteen. One, *Ces Noms* appeared on a busy Toronto street, the names of fourteen women murdered accompanied by the names of fourteen living. Another, *Forever,* consisted of names inscribed on plaques installed in public areas of Winnipeg. "Gibson appropriated the format of patriarchal memorial plaques, customarily used to commemorate men of status. The form is subverted both by the use of names that would be forgotten, were they not the subject of a work of art, and by the inclusion of the pungent phrase 'Murdered by Misogyny,' pointing to an event never before given official recognition."[13]

The names of the women are permanently inscribed on fourteen granite benches arranged in a large circle in Vancouver's Thornton Park, dedicated on December 6, 1997. Each bench is about the length of a woman's body, five and a half feet, and on its surface is a shallow hollow which gathers rainwater, symbolic of tears. The initial impetus behind what is now called *Marker of Change* was Chris McDowell, a Capilano College student at the time of the murders. As is true of many people who made grand gestures in response to the murders, McDowell had "deep personal reasons" for taking action—knowledge of the reality of violence and its consequences. The sheer number of those murdered was critical: "I had dealt with the murders and rapes of women and children one at a time up to that point, but because so many women were murdered at once … I really went down." The way to get back up was through the creation of the monument. "I could see that what was needed in Canada was a permanent, public memorial marking this event. All you hear is the murderer's name.… We need to name the fourteen women."[14]

The distance between seeing what was needed and its accomplishment was beset with difficulties. Responding to a critique from another women's group about the limitations of naming only the women murdered in Montreal, project organizers formulated a dedication inclusive of *all* women: "*In memory, and in grief for all the women who have been murdered by men. We, their sisters and brothers, remember, and work for a better world. For women of all countries, all classes, all ages, all colours.*" An uproar ensued over three words: "murdered by men." It was insulting to men, tarred them all with the same brush, and depicted every man as a senseless brute, the critics raged. The police were called in to look at some of the protest letters received about the dedication and an RCMP file was started. McDowell feared that the project would cause harm, the very opposite of what was the intended purpose of the piece—to promote healing and change. At several points in time, it looked as if the project would flounder, due to a combination of opposition, funding constraints, and bureaucratic red tape, but it was eventually realized as a result of steadfast commitment and innumerable conversations and debates. After widespread consultation, the words of the dedication were not changed, although the order of the phrasing was. The final dedication read: "*The fourteen women named here were murdered December 6, 1989, University of Montreal. We, their sisters and brothers, remember, and work for a better world. In memory, and in grief for all women who have been murdered by men. For women of all countries, all classes, all ages, all colours.*" The project took seven years to come to fruition, and was supported by some six thousand groups and individuals. Many of the women who worked on the project meet still, because long-lasting bonds were forged in the crucible of controversy.

Marker of Change is a powerful installation, the energy of which emanates through the space that has been created. Art has transformative abilities, says McDowell, "the monument circle embraces us." Her own experience of being at the site over the years of planning, installation, and use is indicative of the potential for change. The site for *Marker of Change* is often described as "a rough part of town," and potential visitors are advised not to go there alone. McDowell's experience is that positive changes have occurred: "We used to go to that park and we were terrified.... Several times I've had threatening things happen with men in that park.... Now, nothing like that happens. Men that you meet talk about their lives, or the memorial. The men that go there are outside of society.... Their lives are so hard, they understand that life is hard, that the massacre represents the hardness, the violence in life—it opens their hearts to some extent. I've been really surprised by the changes at the site.[15]

That changes have been experienced at the memorial would be of no surprise to its designer, Beth Alber. "As a visual artist I believe that art can promote change, hence the name: *Marker of Change*.... I saw it.... I saw people having an emotional experience—they knew it was about something important. It's not about violence. It's about thinking and contemplation and peace. All of that allows you to move in that direction."[16] Alber explains that her work has been described as an anti-monument monument, underlining that the space is intended as an invitation to reflection. "Monuments are traditionally thought of as mostly done about war and men, and mostly they are done in the vertical position. They are stamps on the face of the earth. This one is horizontal and low; it invites you to think differently, to feel differently."

The development of the memorial is followed in a documentary entitled *Marker of Change: The Story of the Women's Monument*. One description of it indicates the trajectory of the video: "Like the monument itself, this vital documentary is intended to provoke a shift in Canadian consciousness from denial to healing to societal change."[17] In documenting the struggle to make the dream of the monument a reality, it also documents that denial is deeply entrenched. In the minds of a vocal minority, it seems, it might be acceptable to name victims of violence; however, the gender of those who are most often the perpetrators must remain occluded.

The occlusion of names for a very different purpose is prominent at another memorial site, *Nave for Fourteen Queens*, inaugurated in Montreal on December 5, 1999. The nave sits in a small park that has been named *Place du 6-Décembre 1989*. The designer, a visual artist named Rose Marie Goulet, was assisted by landscape architect Marie-Claude Robert on a project that could also quite appropriately be described as an anti-monument monument. "The site is a tree-filled square in which a kind of glade has been created. A central walkway—like the nave aisle of a cathedral—traverses the space between seven earthen arcs, each divided into two. The fourteen gentle knolls are crowned with a black granite stone bearing the name of one of the women inset in stainless steel. Walking down the aisle is thus a personal, private, tranquil, and natural journey of memory."[18]

The names of the fourteen women are the central feature of the installation, but they are not readily apparent. It is unfortunate (and revealing) that the name and details of the killer are more readily remembered than the names and stories of those who died. The effort required to remember the names of the women is reproduced visually in the memorial. The letters appear abstract because of the way they were created; in fact, at first, many people do not see letters at all. "The technique is to cut from the materials so you are reading from the emptiness," explained Goulet. "The idea of emptiness is important: the women are not here anymore; there is emptiness around then."[19]

It is the level of viewer engagement that this installation requires that makes it unique. *Nave for Fourteen Queens* is not something that can be appreciated from a distance, as is the case with most such art. In Goulet's words: "You walk through the piece, you are part of it.… When you walk in, people are often showing one another how to read—this is a 'g'; this is an 'e'; this is 'n.' When trying to make out the letters [to yourself] you are calling out the names of the women. After people get into the reading, they go to each of them to know who they were. It is like a prayer."

The importance of naming cannot be underestimated. Recalling the names of the dead is an evocative gesture. We are known by our names; they suggest our individuality and specific histories. Hidden behind them are our hopes and dreams, our relationships, our *lives*. Naming women makes them present symbolically. They cannot be lost to us entirely if we still can speak their names.

Naming men as the instigators of the vast majority of acts of violence against women is equally important. "The collective socio-cultural prohibitions against the naming of men's violence, experienced by individual women at an intensely personal and painful level, are a key factor in the enforcement of patriarchal rule."[20] If patriarchal rule is to be challenged, the means by which it is enforced must first be specified. What is not named cannot be countered.

Numbers

Fourteen names, fourteen graves, fourteen photos, fourteen sets of eyes, fourteen papier-mâché torsos suspended from the ceiling—these were some of the images greeting viewers of Don't Remain Silent, a commemorative art show in Toronto.[21] One poem read: "Fifteen women in the arms of mother Death. / The fifteenth is you."[22]

"Seen against the backdrop of other horrors in the world and against the incalculable number of victims of all sorts of violence, what are fourteen unfortunate young women?… A mere drop of water in the ocean—but a drop that … [splashed] us in the eye."[23] Fourteen is very few, perhaps, but it is also very many. London artist Bernice Vincent describes an epiphanic moment in the process of producing *Fourteen Women* (1995), an eight-and-a-half-metre canvas depicting female engineers. "On a heavily textured canvas of dried plants, the light green silhouettes of the figures are painted holding books and other objects against a backdrop of dark green."[24] "As she did the painstaking work of attaching dried plants and painting the scenes, she reached one of those mind-boggling moments when she said to herself, 'Look at how many people I'm painting. It must have been … a bloodbath.'"[25] "The grassy appearance of the surface resembles the ground, but the upright position of the mural reflects the potential growth and vitality that Vincent sees in the women."[26] "The piece isn't about anger," Vincent maintains. "Or about the assault on the women.… It's about loss; about what we lost in those young women, and their potential, just suddenly taken away from us."[27]

The representation of fourteen—fourteen graves, fourteen chairs, fourteen engineers—points to both the many and the one. The many is composed of distinct, unique persons—each has a story, each continues to occupy space. At the annual vigil at Brescia University College in London, fourteen empty chairs serve as a centrepiece, reserving a space for the missing bodies of the women; it is an absence that renders them present. By *his* actions, the murderer said: "There is no place for you here. No place for women at this school." By *ours*, we say the opposite: "Our place is here. It will not be denied to us."

Of course, we cannot lose sight of the fact that the numbers of violent acts against women are growing, and publicity around those numbers receives much less air time than the murders in Montreal still do. December 6 shocked many of us from our lethargy because of the sheer number of those who had been murdered, but also because the victims were in a situation of privilege. Canada's worst one-day mass murder was front-page news for an extended time. Maggie Helwig, a well-known Canadian writer, points out that in some respects the massacre was a "media-friendly" event. "It was sensational; it was fast; they were able to get some visuals.… It wasn't in a private place—this erupted into the public space of the university."[28] Most of the people named on the list of women and children killed in Ontario on an annual basis, compiled by a group which calls itself "Women We Honour," have not made the front pages; only high-profile "domestic incidents" or violators with more than one victim count as news.

"Who counts" is a critical issue here. Rita Beiks is a Vancouver-based artist and member of the Vancouver Women's Monument Committee who began to learn about the violence in the area in which the monument is located while working on the project. Scores of women have disappeared from Vancouver's Downtown Eastside, many murdered. The majority are indigenous women, some of whom were drug addicts and/or sex-trade workers. Not until quite recently has a concerted police effort been made to find the perpetrators. In 1997, Beiks initiated a project with a small group of women, from the local women's centre, who took pictures of their lives over a period of five weeks. "There were pictures of women who were street workers, who were addicts, who were violent themselves," Bieks explains. There were pictures of children, homes, and pets. Looking for themes in the more than five hundred images captured, a message emerged: "These are my friends, this is where I live, this is my home, and these people matter;… we matter; we don't deserve to be brushed aside." A transit shelter poster and a series of mini posters were created. In Beiks' words: "The message on the large transit shelter poster was 'she counts'; there was the image of a woman who had been beaten up, and in the background, a list of the names of all the women that are missing and had died violent deaths. The idea was to play out 'she counts'—the list is growing, we're still counting, we matter."[29]

Martin Dufresne, of Montreal Men Against Sexism, is also counting. He has compiled the names of women killed by men since December 6, 1989, in excess of seven hundred by 2003. It is painstaking work: "I go into libraries, take the tabloids, go day after day, check out the murders, take down the relevant information. I have a paragraph on each case. I look up what happens at trial, what arguments are put forward. I build a synopsis of each case to elicit the gender angle and the extent to which social institutions are complicitious."

On an annual basis the names of the women are published, alphabetized by first name to foster a sense of identification with the victims. The numbers alone make the scope of the problem abundantly clear. One of the earliest comments Dufresne received about the list was from a journalist who knew one of the women on it, and he knew of others who did also. He intuited that eventually it would come to a point where everybody could relate to at least one of the names.[30] Shall we wait for that to happen?

Naming names and keeping count are ways by which we keep memory alive. Memory is quite literally a life-line; it links us to our own histories and to one another. There are those things we would rather *not* remember, memories of hurt and pain, but they too make up the fabric of our lives, and to forget them would be to forget ourselves and the world around us. "We [try to] survive through amnesia. By not remembering what happened to us," said Andrea Dworkin in an address to women at a mental health conference in Banff. The only way to stop accepting violence as normal "is if we refuse to have amnesia everyday of our lives. If we remember what we know about the world we live in."[31] Remembering the names and the ever increasing numbers of murdered and beaten women stands against the forgetfulness that maintains the myth of a civilized society. Memory is both enemy to complacency and the ground of solidarity, connecting us across time and miles to others who remember also.

Claiming the curse

On the first anniversary of the massacre, the organization A Bunch of Feminists organized *Healing Images*, a month-long art exhibition and symposium in memory of the women in Montreal. One of the Bunch explained: "It's important to take what has historically been harmful, and use it to a positive end. That's why we called ourselves 'A Bunch of Feminists.' That's what Lépine called the women at the Montreal Polytechnique, just before he opened fire."[32] There is dignity in turning to a positive end what is thrown against us. Rather than allowing the social disapprobation attached to the term "feminist" to disempower, the word is claimed and the energy it unleashes channelled to critique and creativity.

"Feminist" is a term that is avoided by many women, largely because of a distorted understanding of what it *means* to be a feminist. That the demonization of feminism in the media and elsewhere has been effective is manifest every time a woman vehemently denies any affiliation with it, and every time it is used to dismiss a woman who claims it. A female student at Ecole Polytechnique responded to a question about feminism at the school with this comment: "A feminist is a woman who wants equal rights but a lot of guys who call you a feminist associate it with the 'tough old hag' image."[33] When feminism is claimed, it points to a justifiable desire for equality. When used as a curse, it is used to undermine women's authority. In this case, "feminist" stands as the inverse of socially constructed femininity, which encourages women to be pliant, not tough, young, not old, and beautiful, not a hag.

When Monique Frize was interviewed for the position of first-ever national chair of women in engineering, a position that was to begin in

December, 1989, she was asked if she was a feminist, and said, "no." "I was afraid of the word 'feminism' myself," she says. In the wake of the murders, Frize worked untiringly to encourage girls and women to consider engineering as a career and analyzed the culture of engineering. "Now that I know what it really means I know that I've been a feminist all my life."[34] Michele Landsberg is a well-known feminist and journalist who wrote for many years for the *Toronto Star.* She embraces the term with an enthusiasm that is quite infectious. "I love that word, feminist; I'm so proud of being a feminist. That's one of the best words there is to me because when I was a kid, that word wasn't around. I was considered insane by the people in my high school…. When the feminist movement came along I said 'where have you been all my life?' I am very happy to be identified with the word."[35]

Claiming anger often accompanies the claiming of the term feminist as a self-descriptor. Anger has been counted among the seven deadly sins, and many of us have been taught that it is especially inappropriate in women. One of the simplest ways to dismiss a woman's point of view is to describe her as "just an angry feminist." Anger is often equated with lack of rationality, which makes it suspect in the Western philosophical tradition we have inherited. "Spirit," "reason" and "man" stand against and superior to "body," "emotion" and "woman." The sharp demarcation and hierarchalization of reason and emotion must be set aside. Given the hideous reality of evil in our world, it is entirely unreasonable *not* to be angry.

Recognizing that emotionality has long been trivialized as a source of moral discernment, feminist theologians assert the value of affectivity as a corrective to disembodied reason. The affective reaction of so many women to the murders in Montreal was treated in the media as nothing more than that; sometimes touching, sometimes disruptive displays of tears and anger. But such affective outpouring is more than reaction. It is the beginning of analysis, the pre-articulation of a crushing sense that something is wrong, the energy and motivation to discover and pursue what is wrong and change it. The unhealthy divorce of emotionality from the chambers of reason serves only the mainstream. A healthy spirituality requires the integration of both affectivity and rationality.

The potential of anger must be recognized. Not the kind of anger that indiscriminately wreaks havoc but anger that is holy, righteous rage. The Raging Grannies are groups of social activist women, and they sometimes help organize, or appear at, commemorative events for December 6. Older women who claim the title boldly, they don flamboyant clothing and raise their voices in songs and shouts of protest. The incongruities shock. Older women tend to be invisible in this society, under-represented in the media and in positions of power, their interests seldom considered. Yet the Raging Grannies insist upon being visible and being heard. Incongruity is written into their term of self-identification. "Raging" is not the adjective one expects to describe "grannies." It is indecorous, unbecoming, unbefitting a lady. Yet there they are, laying claim to rage, rejoicing in it.

Where harm is done, anger is the appropriate response, unleashing an energy that cuts through denial and mobilizes for good. Michele Landsberg remembers first hearing about the massacre: "I was filled with shock and horror and grief that I wouldn't expect. It doesn't always hit me; I'm so used to dealing with gruesome things and I defend myself a little in my writing life, but it was just like a physical blow. I could hardly breathe." Landsberg was asked to do a front-page piece for the following day, and "wrote from the heart about the continuum of violence in our culture." It was by turning her grief into anger that the piece was written. "Anger is my banner.... I am angry at injustice.... and my anger always translates into activism. I am going to *do* something about this!"[36]

In *The Stone Diaries*, Carol Shields writes that our loneliness results from an unwillingness to unleash our inner weather.[37] Anger is one face of that weather. Holy anger is a burning flame that cuts through the lies that pass as appeals to reason, to calm, to passivity. Righteous anger wells up from deep inside and erupts forth, a powerful force that can move one to take action in the world.

> *A good anger acted upon*
> *is beautiful as lightning*
> *and swift with power*
> "A Just Anger," Marge Piercy

Symbol and ritual

Anger alone is insufficient to carry us through the long term. Images of life and hope are needed also. Symbols are evocative; they engage our minds and hearts in ways that words alone cannot. Roses and candles are featured often at vigils and on posters, the roses a symbol of the beauty and brevity of life, candles a light in the darkness. Trees have been planted at several locations across the country as signs of growth and strength. The same earth that received the bodies of the murdered women sustains new life.

Roses, candles, and other such symbols often appear in the context of ritual, formalized actions that evoke a sense of the sacred. At the annual December 6 Ritual of Re-Membering at Brescia University College, for instance, drummers play a measured heartbeat to open the ritual, a beat that swells to a resounding crescendo, then abruptly ceases, reminiscent of the abrupt end to fourteen lives. Their names and the names of others who have died at the hands of men are read as candles are lit. A talk by a local activist, a dance celebrating women's strength and beauty, and reflective music complete the ritual. People gather together in a solemn setting to look back and forward, to *feel* back and forward. The ritual traces a path from the extant to the imagined, from a point of remembering and acknowledging the reality of violence against women and toward a vision of a community united in opposition to it. Ritual has been described as an expression in the microcosm of what we desire in the macrocosm. Brescia's ritual is an assertion of the sacredness of life and a collective expression of abhorrence when that sacredness is violated. It offers participants the possibility of being part of a community of individuals looking together toward the same end. Imagining and experiencing a time when people gather to insist on and defend the sacredness of life can be a source of hope, and hope inspires action.

Rituals trace a journey. A musical ritual is found in the work of Hildegard Westerkamp, a Vancouver-based composer whose "Ecole Polytechnique" for church bells, choir, instruments, and tape was performed in Montreal in November of 1990. One review of the piece called it a "a quasi-documentary," quite appropriately in that it "creates a musical journey through the emotions of what happens in this kind of event."[38] The journey begins with an emotional build-up of tension, and then goes into the event, the horror of it. As a soundscape artist, Westerkamp uses sounds from the environment to evoke an atmosphere. The choir part consists of long tones, breathing, whispering, a scream. There are ominous sounding bells, threatening bird sounds, the sounds of shots and sirens, excerpts from media reports. The music then draws you into the underworld, and "gradually there is a surfacing, the breathing begins again."

In practicing the piece, some choir members expressed unease with it. "Some people thought it was too stirring, it brings everything out again." But the stirring is deliberate. According to Westerkamp, it is important that we have the space to feel something, to "attend to certain things, certain emotions, certain thoughts, certain situations;" to ask: "What is important in life, what do we honour? The shock of someone walking into any space and starting to shoot undermines what's important in our lives, or highlights everything that's important in life. It creates a strange sense of clarity at the same time. As we are closer to birth and death there comes this clarity about what's important."[39] "'Ecole Polytechnique' taps into ancient lamenting traditions, with their cathartic and healing functions that historically served both the individual and the community."[40]

Vigils and rituals serve similar functions, appealing to emotional and spiritual, rather than exclusively rational, sensibilities in an effort to promote healing. Rituals of remembering and memorials are not without controversy, however. Questions are raised about *who* is being remembered, and *to what end*. Routinely on December 7 there is coverage of candles, prayers, and tears. Are these enough?[41] Sharon Rosenberg raises questions about the value of symbolic acts of remembrance insofar as they displace, or substitute for, concrete commitments for change: "How is it that a national day of remembrance, white ribbons, gun control panels, and commissions form the dominant response(s)? What discourses of moral regulation are being privileged so that these 'symbolic' acts of remembrance are in place without / instead of a 'material' commitment to ending violences against women?"[42] The efficacy of annual vigils is questioned also by Nova Scotian artist Regina Coupar, who created a lithograph called *Sacrifice of the Death Cycle* for an anniversary exhibition. Coupar has taken part in several of the yearly remembrances, but finds them increasingly difficult to attend: "I'm not sure what the value is in continuing these. My fear is that the women become idolized and the greater cause suffers. I'm not sure that they're helpful for furthering the larger cause."[43] A statement issued from Vancouver's Downtown Eastside Women's Centre in February 2002 that protested inaction on the part of the police and others to investigate the disappearances of women from the area ended with this: "The police and the government need to take us seriously. One is too many. Fifty is outrageous. We are tired of memorials."[44] Pamela Harrison of Transition House Association of Nova Scotia in Halifax raises questions about using memorials for the fourteen women in Montreal as a way to inform people about more common forms of violence against women. She points out that "in some ways focus on the Montreal Massacre in anniversary events is counterproductive to the kind of work we are doing, to get people to understand it's your next door neighbour who is abusing or being abused.... I'm always nervous of events that are extraordinary being the focus of what are unfortunately very ordinary occurrences."[45]

These are valid cautions; nonetheless, the opportunity to participate in rituals and memorials is important for many people. They provide avenues for connecting with one another and our pasts, but in a way that points us to the future, to the days when memorials for murdered women will be no longer necessary. The very act of gathering with others for comfort is an act of empowerment; the term "comfort" is derived from the Latin for *com* and *fort:* to fill with strength. "We need the candlelight vigils and concerts for Dec. 6 just as we need the solemn bells and silences of Nov. 11," writes Michele Landsberg. "We need the cleared space, the stopping of time's relentless clock, the ceremony and the heightened words that will unlock our feelings and make us remember."[46] Clearly, remembering alone is insufficient, but without it there will be no concerted demands for material, systemic change.

Mobilization

Women and men across the country sprang into action in the wake of the murders. One of the most visible organizational efforts was the gun-control lobby spearheaded by Heidi Rathjen (a Polytechnique student in the building the evening of December 6) and Wendy Cukier, a professor at Ryerson University in Toronto. A coalition consisting of families of the murdered women and people from public health, crime prevention, and religious and community organizations, among others, have continued to press for stricter gun laws. Hundreds of organizations and individuals contributed to the effort. Peter Davison, co-founder of Halifax's Men for Change, took a different approach. A heightened awareness of the pervasiveness of men's violence toward women after December 6 brought him to the realization that "there are three types of men: men who use violence to solve problems, men who remain silent when it happens, and men who speak up to try and make a change. I wanted to be part of a group of men who cared enough to be recognized and identified as people who were attempting to understand the complexities of violence and do our small part to end sexism and violence against women."

One of the initiatives of Men for Change was the development of the Healthy Relationships curriculum, a violence prevention program for teenagers. "For us a direct call and a very sensible outcome of the Montreal Massacre, to turn that craziness and pain into something that made sense, was to commit ourselves to speak about our experiences as men and to transfer that into a program for people we might never meet," says Davison. The program has been adopted internationally, most notably by Juvenile Courts and Community Schools division of the Los Angeles County Office of Education in California, a division teaching sixty thousand incarcerated juveniles a year. "From the Montreal Massacre affecting a small men's group in Nova Scotia to reaching out to help with the problem of gang violence in California. The ripple effect, the waves of hope, in teaching nonviolence and healthy masculinity that started because of the Montreal Massacre have been quite remarkable."[47]

The White Ribbon Campaign has also elicited considerable response. This organization of men working to end men's violence against women is now the largest such organization in the world. The campaign encourages men and boys to wear a white ribbon as a pledge to help eradicate violence against women, provides educational resources to schools across Canada and the States, and raises funds for women's groups. Columnist Michele Landsberg describes it as "one of the more dramatically successful advocacy campaigns on 'women's issues' that I've ever seen."[48] The irony of the success of the White Ribbon campaign has not been lost on many feminists who have tried for years to raise awareness and funds with meager results. The privilege and status afforded to white male professionals is translated in this case into widespread and generous support of what is now an international cause. In some places the White Ribbon Campaign has impinged on similar campaigns initiated by women. The Purple Ribbon Campaign in Nova Scotia is a case in point. In 2001, the organizers of the campaign "wrote to the White Ribbon Campaign in Toronto and asked them to step back in Nova Scotia. We can't get corporate sponsorship when they move in. They are a national organization with national sponsorship.... They have the glossy presentations.... While we don't want to discourage men being part of the process we just don't want them doing it at the same time."[49]

Mobilizing in a different way, Monique Frize took on the engineering profession. She was about to take up her position as the first holder of a national chair of women in engineering when she heard about the murders. "It changed my life and my work completely, from being in gear one to gear five." The first day of her job she attended the funeral of some of the victims in Montreal. "I was with two other women, and I said to them "a thousand women for every one that died. I was so angry.... And ten years later we had fifteen thousand more women engineers." For several years Frize visited hundreds of schools, did countless media interviews, spoke about women and engineering to students, professors, deans and decision makers, parents and teachers. Frize has been relentless in promoting engineering as a career choice for women and in her critiques of the culture of engineering as well. "I won't be shut up any more. They gave me a microphone and I'm using it."[50]

Working in a smaller, but just as crucial, frame, the December 6 Coalition is a volunteer organization in the Greater Toronto area that provides small, interest free loans to women leaving abusive situations. Originally set up to organize commemorative events, it now provides loans to about one hundred women annually for such things as rent deposits, moving expenses, telephones—the practical things that make the move to independence possible. According to Jane Kostner, co-founder of the organization, "The issue of violence has been studied to death. We know what it does to women and children. The fund is material help. You have to start somewhere."[51]

These and many other mobilizing efforts are all instances of "starting somewhere." They begin with the urge to act, to take the initiative and effect some change in the world. They might even be described as acts of faith. The belief that the face of the world can and must change is focused in a particular direction by some brave few, picks up momentum, and eventually touches thousands of lives. Many people feel powerless before the broad range and pervasiveness of injustice and inequality that characterize the contemporary world. A conviction that individuals *can* effect change is an act of faith in the power of individual will and collective action. We are not simply at the mercy of other people, institutions, and patterns of social and economic organizations. We are not helpless before them, hopeless before them. The will and agency of people working in concert to effect change on a variety of fronts is a tribute to the human spirit, a spirit that does not cower and that grows stronger in the doing.

A Spirituality of Resistance

These recurring motifs and strategies can be described as particular manifestations of a spirituality of resistance. They are evidence of a will to life, which at its most basic is what "spirituality" signifies. "Feminist theologian Ursula King ... describes women's spirituality as 'a struggle for life.' ... Spirituality is not separate from women's lives and experiences, but deeply interwoven with women's struggles for survival, including resisting and overcoming violence. She defines spirituality as a force for survival, an inspiring resource in our struggle and resistance, a powerful tool, and a method of transformation."[52]

To inquire into spirituality is to ask: What does it take to live? Many people experienced the massacre as a blow to the spirit. In Maggie Helwig's poem "Flashpoint," "he says die," is a recurring refrain. "He says / Die / Die / they say / die...." and something did die in many of us. But the murderer cannot have the last word. He says die, but "we must keep on living if we can."[53] "Spirituality" points to the inner resources necessary to sustain us in the long, arduous struggle for life. If we are to keep on living in the face of tragedy, violence, and outrage, we need to engage in actions that express our anguish and both sustain and fire our spirits.

While "resistance is lived in culturally and historically specific ways,"[54] it is possible to refer in general terms to the *characteristics* of a spirituality of resistance. The kinds of actions in which women and men engaged in response to the horror of December 6 suggest that such a spirituality is (at least) *bi-dimensional*; it is both a movement *against* and a movement *toward*. Resistance is by definition oppositional. Those who resist stand up against whatever threatens to overwhelm them; they push back; they plant themselves firmly and say: Enough! Here, resistance takes the form of outrage against the murderous act itself and also at efforts to isolate and decontextualize it. While resistance *is* oppositional, it is not restricted to negation and contradiction. Resistance does say "No!" denouncing violence against women in all its forms, but at the same time it says "Yes!"—Yes to exuberant, abundant life. This is opposition by way of hope; it writes hope over despair, empowerment over hopelessness; it opposes by envisioning an alternative. A spirituality of resistance looks both forward and back. It has a long specific memory that refuses to forget the history of violence done to women, but does not get mired there. Anger and tears are translated into action for social change.

The bi-dimensional character of a spirituality of resistance is made apparent by the initiatives that sought to establish some permanent memorial or legacy related to the massacre, and those in which impermanence was seen of value. Elaine Carol, member of A Bunch of Feminists, prepared a fifteen-minute performance piece entitled "Mark Lépine thought he was a hero in uniform." Carol played three parts in a once-only performance around the first anniversary of the massacre: Lépine, a mourning mother, and a female engineering student who had survived the carnage She refers to such one-time pieces as "dangerous performances." They are memorial pieces which, like a eulogy or funeral, are enacted once and never again—"that's what lasts."[55] Impermanence is also central to Hildegard Westerkamp's "Ecole Polytechnique," a musical piece commissioned for church bells which ran the risk of never being performed at all. Because of the bells the performance had to be held outdoors. It was scheduled for early November in Montreal, a time when inclement weather was a distinct possibility and would require cancelling the event. Three thousand people attended the once-only performance on what was a very mild day. The next day it started snowing. What those who heard the piece are left with is their memory of it.

A spirituality of resistance is *engaged*. Much of what passes for spirituality at a popular level involves learning to gracefully and gratefully accept what has been given to us. It endorses an embrace of ourselves and our lives, inner peace amid the turmoil of daily life, and an ability to accept with equanimity whatever comes our way. A spirituality of resistance resists an easy, or even hard-won, acquiescence. It seeks not to reconcile with the world but to change it. This challenges long-held understandings of spirituality that perceive a divorce between spirituality and activism. Traditional notions of spirituality have been shaped by a dualistic paradigm that separates spirit and matter, soul and body, sacred and profane, heaven and earth, and values the former aspect of each pairing above the latter. From this vantage point, spirituality has to do with otherworldly aspirations—it looks upward, heavenward, elsewhere, and certainly away from the base realities of our daily lives. In contrast, the kind of spirituality described here refuses such artificial distinctions. It is a spirituality "conceptually inseparable from liberatory action that addresses the material conditions of people's lives."[56] It implies not a quieting of the soul, but its awakening—an awakening to injustice, to the necessity of putting one's own body in the breach. A spirituality of resistance is not passive and otherworldly, but is immersed in *this* world, moving toward transforming both individual consciousness and social structures.

A spirituality of resistance is *polyvalent*, manifest in a variety of forms, on many fronts. It is carried in protest, solidarity, and anger, made manifest in word and art, in ritual, in voices raised together. It is a complex spirituality that works on a variety of levels of consciousness—linear and logical, creative and imaginative. No one mode of expression can ever begin to express what we experience as reality. Words on a page, or sprayed on a wall, convey meaning that impacts the reader in a particular way. She meets words with words. Art and music often meet with a different level of response. Carol Ann Weaver's "Fourteen Women/Quatorze Femmes,"an eighteen-minute musical piece, originally played by a fourteen-person ensemble, is a musical journey through life and death that has transformative potential. "Music can express things which are subconscious, superconscious, unconscious, sensually conscious, not necessarily rationally conscious. And when that kind of consciousness is tapped a person can be altered. It is like tapping into another kind of river of life.... Music reaches way beyond the rational, the deepest limits.... To me, it's the closest I can get to God, to my sense of God—it allows us to dip into a place that is as purely spirit as I know within the forms of expression we have."[57]

Polyvalence as a characteristic points to the fact that there is not one best way to understand or act. There is sometimes a rift perceived between those who engage in political action (government, law, economics) and those who focus on spiritual pursuits that are more symbolically oriented (culture, art, music, literature, language, mythology and religion).[58] I have gathered both orientations—from lobbying relentlessly for improvements in gun control laws to annual memorials in which candles are lit for murdered women—under the same umbrella, as manifestations of a spirituality of resistance. Those who resist the term "spirituality" may well object, and on grounds well founded. Historically, spirituality has largely discounted the material world in which we live and move and have our beings. A spirituality of resistance does not. Embracing both political activism and symbolic acts and sites memorializing murdered women serves to highlight the wide spectrum of activities that must be engaged to address the issue. Legislative changes alone are insufficient, because the roots of violence are grounded in culture and language as well as regulatory bodies. Symbolic acts alone are insufficient, because it will take more than an appeal to a transformed consciousness to transform social structures. Both approaches are needed, working in concert. The Dalai Lama has been asked this: "if enough people meditate, will that save the world?" His answer: "If we wish to save the world, we must have a plan. But unless we meditate, no plan will work." Our spiritual work increases our personal power and thus our effectiveness in the world. Our political work is an expression of our inner lives; it points to what we consider ultimate in life; it is evidence of a will to life, which, in the final analysis, is the very heart of spirituality.

"Polyvalence" also recognizes that there are significant tensions and ambiguities in responses to December 6. Many individuals understood it as the extreme end of a continuum of violence, while others objected to using the massacre to symbolize violence against women because its specific features were thereby obscured. It is more often the case that the perpetrator of violence is known to the victim, an intimate, in fact, rather than some stranger who walks in off the street. The issue of identifying with the Ecole Polytechnique victims is also a matter of contention. Many women responded with this: "It could have been me. It could have been my daughter." What such remarks make clear in contrast are the many women with whom we do *not* identify. The massive response to the murders had to do with the sheer numbers, but also with the fact that those killed were middle-class white women at a university, not prostitutes on the street, and not women in abusive relationships, whose affairs are largely presumed to be domestic and personal. Why were *these* fourteen women the focus of such attention when so many other victims go unacknowledged? There is a racial and class bias in some women's identification with the women in Montreal. Can we come to identify equally with sex-trade workers from Vancouver's East end who have disappeared and been murdered? Here is where the extent of our compassion is measured. To be compassionate is to "feel with." Those with whom we feel must be greatly expanded if any effective challenges to the patriarchal/hierarchical structure in which we live are to be mounted.

These and other such tensions cannot be dismissed or underplayed. They issue a challenge to hold at one time both the specificity and uniqueness of December 6, and its status as emblematic of ongoing violence against women. That is no easy task, but one that is more respectful of the complexities of life and death. "There is always more than one underlying truth," says Martin Dufresne, "and there is always movement in opposite directions at the same time."[59]

A spirituality of resistance is *visionary.* Implicit within the responses surveyed here is a belief that current realities are transformable, even when seemingly intransigent, and a vision of a future substantially different from the present. Lois Wilson, former Moderator of the United Church of Canada, writes that we live in two worlds simultaneously, one presumed and one proposed. The presumed one is the one we look out upon, a world of suffering and violence. The proposed world does not deny these realities, but includes a vision of those realities transformed. "The proposed world is a world of mutuality, inclusive community, equity, and justice we can only imagine. But we should never underestimate the power of the world of visions and imagination...." The task is to communicate our vision of a proposed world and then move into it.[60]

Our visions and dreams of a world transformed are partially realized in creative acts that anticipate that world. Mahatma Gandhi is often quoted as saying: "You must *be* the change you wish to see in the world." A variant on this—*make* the change you wish to see—is evident in another of Rita Beiks's art pieces to mark December 6. In 1995, Beiks was concerned that the initial outrage had faded and the media was not doing enough to mark the day. Calls to the papers and media did not elicit any promise to do more, so Beiks decided to do it herself. She created a mock-up of the *Globe and Mail's* Report on Business. "All the headlines were about violence against women, trade stories were about human rights practices, I did a dream column about what I'd like to see happening in business." Beiks and some friends placed a thousand copies in papers at the Vancouver Stock Exchange. "It had an effect, got a lot of attention. It was a way to get the media to talk about what I wanted them to talk about. They weren't doing it on their own and they certainly weren't doing it because I asked them to do it."[61]

"Art is a source and a repository of vision.... Feminists can create art which bridges gaps between the society around us and the one we hope to bring into existence."[62] So too can music, theology, ritual, and activism bridge the gap between what *is* and what *is desired.* According to Baum, "redemption from structural sin begins with graced individuals enabled to see clearly, to resist, to communicate and to organize."[63] The individuals represented here are so graced; they are visionaries who share their visions and act on them. They are sustained by a spirituality that illuminates life, that sees beyond what is in their immediate range of vision. Their fire within is a flame that lights the way forward for those of us willing to take the journey with them.

The Road Out

"For me, writing something down is the only road out."

— Anne Tyler

What "road out" is suggested by the many and diverse initiatives described above: the art, the music, the activism, the organizing? It is at least three-fold, and includes recognition, which entails facing unflinchingly the realities of our lives, opposition to the brutalities that desecrate them, and various modes of reconsecration.

Recognition of the pervasiveness of violence in our society is difficult and painful; one risks descent into madness. Who can face the sheer number of murders and assaults, the incest, the pornography, the "reign of sexist terror"?[64] If faced, there is both danger and possibility. Recognition unleashes anger that can be directed inward or out. Turned in, it can lead to despair and hopelessness. Directed outward, it can turn into an attack or it can be channelled into creative, combative efforts to promote change. Engaging in oppositional activity—resisting the violence in some form or other—can itself be fraught with peril. Some of the people who have been introduced here, including Martin Dufresne, Wendy Cukier, members of the Vancouver Women's Monument Committee, and organizers of the December 6 ritual at Brescia University College, have received threats. Efforts to resist violence are sometimes met with violence. A resilient spirit is needed to sustain us in the face of such opposition.

Our lives are desecrated by violence, their holy essence denied. They need to be reconsecrated, their holiness affirmed. Musicians such as Hildegard Westerkamp and Carol Ann Weaver evoke this musically. Weaver's "Fourteen Women/Quatorze Femmes" takes one on a journey, from the energy of the lives of the women, through the "frozen landscape" of their deaths, to "a sublime kind of sense of their spirits coming back to bless us, as it were."[65] Of her "Ecole Polytechnique," Westerkamp says: "I cannot remain silent about the Montreal Massacre and the impact it had on myself and many others. I want to 'talk back' to it. I also want to make room to heal, to hope, to transform energies, and to understand the work that is ahead of us. I invite all listeners … to listen inward and search for what is sacred,… what cannot be allowed to be killed inside us."[66] In the face of death we affirm life—this is the ultimate act of resistance.

Throughout this chapter I have used the term "resistance" in a positive light and in relation to gestures that oppose violence and insist on life over death. There are, of course, other forms of resistance which are not life-giving. Witness the event that initiated this project: the murderous resistance of one man to advances made by women in an engineering school. Witness the fierce resistance to rather moderate changes in gun-control laws. Witness the growing rise of the men's and father's rights movement. Witness too the resistance to real changes in social relations, such as is manifest in negative reactions to pay equity policies. The kinds of changes that have been more readily embraced in terms of violence against women after December 6 have been largely symbolic, if not entirely without controversy. Events calling for reflection and remembrance—vigils, memorials, art, and music—are generally well received (unless they exclude men or refer specifically to gendered violence). Calls for more fundamental changes are more strenuously, and institutionally, resisted.

The kinds of responses that I have classified under a "spirituality of resistance" are by and large those which stand against the ideological practices described in the previous chapter, practices which prevent us from knowing what we know, masking relations of domination, disorganizing our ability to make connections, and inhibiting the possibility of collective action. The initiatives described here do precisely the opposite. They uncover relations of domination, expand our ability to make connections, and promote the possibility of collective action. I return to the question that opened this chapter: What shall we tell our bright and shining daughters? Tell them we're fighting back.

Conclusion: Look Again

We trod a weary path through silent woods,
Tangled and dark, unbroken by a sound
Of cheerful life. The melancholy shriek
Of hollow winds careering o'er the snow,
Or tossing into waves the green pine tops,
Making the ancient forest groan and sigh
Beneath their mocking voice, awoke alone
The solitary echoes of the place.
— Susanna Moodie, *Roughing It in the Bush*

A journey motif and cartography—an attempt to map a way through the entanglement of responses to the Montreal Massacre—have been themes throughout this work. Susanna Moodie provides a model. Moodie met this country bravely; she struggled with cold and loss and want, but did not shrink from the challenge of making a home in an unfriendly, at times malicious, land. She managed with good hard work, making use of all the tools at her disposal. And she wrote, undoubtedly one of the means through which she maintained her sanity.

The tools at my disposal are many: Gregory Baum, who writes about the theological imperative to name our realities; Dorothy Smith, who provides a means of doing precisely that; theologians, poets, artists, musicians, activists, and years of thought, commentary, and action around a violent event that has had a profound impact on many Canadians. Much ground has been covered. I have referred to newspapers, academic journals, documentaries, poetry, and art exhibits. I have wrestled with theology, sociology, interdisciplinary relationships, media practices, and government policies. I have taken twenty horrific minutes, sixteen years of responses, and written, appropriating whatever was useful to open up even one small portion of the complex of relations that shape our lives. So have I arrived here. And well the quintessentially Canadian question might be asked: Where is here?[1]

Here is needing to go on.

The structure of this extended reflection gives the impression of linearity, moving from this point to that, ever forward. But the reality is somewhat different, more circular. While it is true that there has been a substantial shift in the characterization of the murders toward a more widespread understanding of them as part of a continuum of violence against women, the violence continues, and many of the original responses continue to be replayed. There is still the urge to silence (keep quiet, and everything will be fine), still the myth of a civilized society tragically interrupted by occasional aberrant behavior, still the suspicion that women cause the violence done to them, still the lack of widespread questioning of the structural supports for violence against women. Ongoing too are the lobbying around gun control, the mandating of yet more studies and reports, the tendency to see particular acts of violence as discrete, and solutions in individualized treatment. Controversies of signification continue as well, both over the meaning of the murders themselves and over the meaning and efficacy of various memorials of them.

Christina Benson's comments in December 1990 are no less true today: "Canadian women are regularly beaten up, assaulted, abused, harassed at home and in the workplace, mutilated, and killed. Reportage of this is given momentary and fleeting coverage and treated in a sensational manner without any context of systematic analysis. A rhetoric of bureaucratic and government effort exists to address the issue but it is evasively diffuse." Her further observations are quite chilling: "In Canada, we practice a rhetoric of awareness and concern that in fact places women at greater risk than a coldly admitted tolerance for violence would do. If we claim that the problem does not exist, or that if it exists it is minor, we psychologically place women in distress, as they attempt to reconcile their personal experiences and perceptions with official rhetoric."[2] Note well: If we let down our vigilance, resting in the assurance that as a nation we are dealing valiantly with violence against women *because we say that we are,* we put women in harm's way.

Margaret Atwood's *The Journals of Susanna Moodie* ends with a resurrected Moodie travelling in "A Bus Along St. Clair: December." "What does [she] come back to tell us? The careful order of walls and ceilings, of wires and a 'silver paradise,' cannot deny the insistent reality of wilderness."[3]

> Turn, look down:
> there is no city;
> This is the centre of a forest.[4]

Violence against women has not ceased, and neither has our capacity to resist and create alternatives. Having taken this journey, it is clear that these paths will be trod many times again.

Here is a strategic theology.

Paying attention to the particulars and politics of where we are is the strategy that has been followed in these pages. This is a revelatory strategy that intends to incite action. Theology has often been described as "faith seeking understanding." Reordering the terms to describe theology as "understanding seeking faith" serves to highlight the struggle to have and keep faith, given the world in which we live, but either definition emphasizes the ongoing, dynamic nature of theology. Theology is a process. It is not static, not the dissemination of eternal truths, for instance, but active and searching, if never fully finding.

I agree with Beverly Harrison when she writes that "the dominant theological language and images of western theology have lost their capacity to elicit spontaneous, dynamic, imaginative power,... [and] reveal an immense conventionality and repetitiveness."[5] Beginning theological reflection in the actual rather than the conceptual has the capacity to unleash imaginative power and compel movement forward. We begin where we are and must be, in the actualities of our lives. Attention to the mundane does not prescind from actual experiences of life, of relationality, of sin and grace. Such attention cracks open what is hidden and has caused despair—it *reveals.* A focus on everyday life and experience makes action a necessity, not a moral choice or option. In coming to recognize the extent, dimension and causes of oppression we acquire a consciousness which forces us by "an ineluctable distress"—by practical necessity—

to revolt against inhumanity.[6] Action becomes necessary, and solidarity with others possible. Oppression is not experienced in the abstract. It is experienced in the flesh, in broken bones, and lives lost. So too grace. It is devoid of content until it becomes manifest in specific acts that write life over death. It is herein that the divine is revealed. It is that longing, that pull to life, that draws us outward, forward, and toward one another. That which is sacred wells up from deep within; it moves through the eyes in tears, through the mouth in shouts and whispers, through the arms in gestures of protest and embrace. It moves the heart to break and heal. It moves the feet forward, refusing to stand still. When we weep with the precariousness of life, the divine is revealed. When we seek to restore that which is damaged and broken, the divine is revealed. That which is sacred is made manifest in every act and word and image that mourns the pain we cause one another and acknowledges the truth of who we are: flawed and wanting, always wanting more.

Grounding theology in particulars is revelatory insofar as light is shed on the concrete conditions in which we live and on that which is sinful and sacred therein. It is also revolutionary, in that theology is recast. "A theologian who works within the horizon of specific manifestations of sin, whether racism, sexism, or militarism, finds herself or himself reshaping the very categories of theological reflection."[7] In the analysis developed here, there have been no references to grand theory, no discussion of human nature, no mention of the characteristics of a redeemed world. Instead of putting forth an abstract argument for justice, the concrete conditions which deny justice are analyzed.[8] Rather than evoking an all-embracing faith that calls for a new world, that which makes it possible to resist is recognized.[9] There can no longer be grand theological systems, comprehensive, all-encompassing theologies produced by lone giants in ancient castles. There *can* be solidarities, partnerships, and responses to specific forms of oppression. As Michel Foucault so elegantly states: In our time the intellectual is "no longer the rhapsodist of the eternal, but the strategist of life and death."[10]

Here is a question: Whence change?

And now, sixteen years later, twenty, twenty-five, what has changed? Much. It is vitally important to identify and celebrate the changes that have occurred in the wake of December 6—reforms at engineering schools, the establishment of centres to study violence, the national day of remembrance and action on violence against women, the memorial art and sites that keep memory alive, and the very many other initiatives that have been launched. But can we point to signs of fundamental social transformation, a phrase often used by liberation theologians to point to the radical changes in social structures and organization that would make for a just and equitable world? Unfortunately not. Or, more optimistically, not yet.

How does fundamental social change happen? It certainly does not inevitably follow from a shift in understanding, although consciousness-raising is unquestionably a necessary precursor. More than an acknowledgment that violence is pervasive and must be curbed is necessary. *Awareness* of the reality of violence against women must be accompanied by an *analysis* of the many forms it takes and the societal, institutional, and attitudinal supports for it. Sociologist Anthony Giddens writes that sociological analysis can play an emancipatory role "by showing that what may appear to those involved as inevitable, as unchallengeable—as resembling a law of nature—is, in fact, an historical product."[11] The social order is a historical product, a human product, and, as such, it is within the realm of human possibility to modify that product, even transform it. In theological terms, we share in the ongoing creation of the world.

Even this is insufficient, particularly if analysis leads one to a sense of powerlessness in the face of the enormity of the problem and the magnitude of the mandate. The best analysis in the world will not necessarily call forth the will to engage in the concerted actions necessary for social transformation. *Belief* must accompany analysis, belief in the power of human agency to effect change. This is a leap of faith in many ways, but a leap that can be attempted if there is sufficient evidence showing that individuals *do* have power that can challenge the powers that oppress. It is imperative that we remember that a history of oppression is also a history of resistance that must be recalled and celebrated. Acts of resistance to violence carry "marks of dignity, courage, and potential," and foregrounding them can help to sustain our faith that we participate in shaping the world.

The belief that we share in the work of creation is meaningless if that work is not actively and passionately engaged. A *commitment to action* is necessary. It is possible to maintain faith in this broken world only through continual, creative engagement in it. Long-lasting change will take the concerted effort of committed people, working on many different fronts, who will not necessarily agree that any particular front is a worthy one: lobbies, rituals, marches, music, articles, art, civil disobedience, prayer, work-shops, theatre, boycotts, books, memorials, Web pages, protests, petitions, poetry, coalitions, studies, posters, alternative communities, campaigns, law-making, law-breaking, tea parties, and guerilla tactics. There are no small gestures. Every time we say no to violence—challenge a sexist com-ment, refuse pornography, support a women's shelter—at the very least, we ourselves are changed. The accumulation of changes, at individual and community levels, will effect discernible social change. Given the multi-tudinous forms that violence takes and the regulatory, religious, economic, and cultural institutions that sanction it, efforts to combat violence must take many forms.

Needed also, a long view. It will take more than my lifetime, more than yours, to effect the kinds of changes that will make Canada an unambigu-ously safe and welcoming place for women. It will take our good hard work, our commitments, and our vision of a just world, and it will also take longer than we have as individuals. This is overly daunting unless we share an unwavering conviction that life is longer than we are.[12] Michele Landsberg has said that the Jewish concept *tikkun olam*—repair of the bro-ken world—is her watchword. Rabbi Tarfon taught: "It is not your respon-sibility to finish the work [of perfecting the world], but you are not free to desist from it either."[13]

Here is back again.

Alice Munro concludes her story "The Ottawa Valley" with the "statement that 'if [she] had been making a proper story' it would have ended differ-ently. She has resisted the land of closure which works toward an illu-sory illumination, she explains, because 'she wanted to find out more.'"[14] Wanting to find out more has been the heart and drive of this book, want-ing to know how it works, how it happens, how it might be changed. Inquiry of this kind is open-ended, resisting illusory closure. "It is like the making of a quilt that remains to be attached to other pieces in the cre-ation of a whole pattern."[15] The pattern emerges only in the doing, in working for a world more just and whole, and in finding out more. As Gwendolyn MacEwan wrote:

> Do not imagine that the exploration
> ends, that she has yielded all her mystery

or that the map you hold
cancels further discovery

... look again
(burn your maps, that is not what I mean),
I mean the moment when it seems most plain
is the moment when you must begin again.[16]

Appendix

For me, writing something down is the only road out.   — Anne Tyler

Here is an invitation.

Writing itself can be an expression of resistance. It is an act of creation, of expression. It says "I have something to say. I will not be silent. I cannot be silent." Writing can provide a clarity and focus, even direction. According to author Deena Metzger, "The muse urges us toward service; the muse, when she appears, takes us out of our little life and thrusts us into the world."[1]

The writing exercises below provide opportunities to engage your own reflective and creative processes. The first, "Writing against Forgetting," is a version of a reflection prepared at the invitation of a member of the Ursuline Community based in Chatham, Ontario, and appeared in their newsletter on the tenth anniversary of the December 6 murders. If those who died in Montreal in 1989 are not first and foremost on your horizon when considering the fact of violence, adapt the instructions to foreground the woman who is. The second, "Five Lines," is a poetic exercise that was made available to participants at Brescia University College's fourteenth Ritual of Remembrance. After the ceremony itself, those so inclined were led through a simple guided poetry exercise, laid out in Maria Harris's *Dance of the Spirit*. Remarkably many women *were* so inclined. As Margaret Atwood says, "a word after a word after a word is power."[2] The third exercise, "What I Know," asks you to consider the wisdom that you possess, and to put that wisdom to work.

Rapid free writing is the recommended technique. Write continuously for a short period of time, without stopping, without even thinking overly much, in response to the particular prompt. The continuous and non-reflective character of the exercise allows the writer to tap into the unconscious. Most of the writing we engage in on a regular basis is the product of much deliberation, the weighing out of different options, choosing this word or that, censoring, in fact, most of what is thought in favour of some measure of coherence. When incoherence is permitted—embraced—hidden depths may come to light.

Writing against Forgetting

Anniversaries are a time for remembering, for looking both forward and back. Let's look with pen in hand. There are three prompts below designed to help access your memories and musings. Before beginning each exercise, take a moment to stop, breathe, and focus. A moment's deliberation can be sufficient to create a sense of silence and purpose within you. After pausing, begin to write down whatever rises to the surface of consciousness. Write continuously for fifteen to twenty minutes, without stopping, without censoring. If you get stuck, write about being stuck until you can gently refocus. Following your pen across a page can lead to places deep within.

Remember ...

On December 6, 1989, a gunman entered an engineering school in Montreal and murdered fourteen women. Years later, the echo of the gunshots still reverberate in the hearts and memories of each of us. Remembering is an act of resistance. Remembering the names and the ever increasing numbers of murdered and beaten requires a response: "No more and never again." Memory is both enemy to complacency and the ground of solidarity, connecting us across time and miles to others who remember also.

Write "I remember" at the top of a page, and record a memory associated in whatever way with the event and its aftermath. Don't edit; simply write down whatever bubbles to the surface in as much detail as possible. When one particular memory is exhausted, write "I remember" again, and proceed from there.

If your tears could speak ...

When the seemingly unthinkable happens, the body often responds before the mind engages. Where did you *feel* the news that fourteen women had been brutally murdered? In eyes brimming over with tears? In clenched hands? In a convulsing gut? Take a few moments to remember your body's response. Then be attentive to the way your body is responding *right now*— it knows in ways your mind cannot.

If your tears (or hands or gut) could speak to you, what would they say? Record what you hear, letting words, like tears, well forth.

What can we say ...

"They are so precious to us, our daughters," began Stevie Cameron, writing shortly after the massacre of fourteen women in Montreal. "We tell our bright, shining girls that they can be anything.... But as they grow and learn, with aching hearts we have to start dealing with their bewilderment about injustice.... What can we say to our bright and shining daughters?"[3] What *can* we say to our bright and shining daughters? Hold in your mind and heart a woman or girl who is precious to you. What do you need to say to her—about aching hearts, about love, about what we need to do to make things work, about anything at all? You have twenty minutes to write down everything you need to share. Write quickly; time is passing.

Afterword

Spending an hour alone with pen in hand is a solitary activity but not done alone. The words on your page are part of a collective lament: one breath in a sigh that rises up to heaven; one breath in a howl that fills the sky. Our memories, outrage, and hope merge with those of every other woman who looks back to the horror of December 6, 1989, and forward in anticipation to a world where our bright and shining daughters are truly cherished.

Five Lines

Upon completion of this exercise, you will have written a cinquain, a five-line stanza. Simply follow the directions. Suggestions for the one-word subject that constitutes the first line were provided for participants at Brescia's annual Ritual of Remembering. They included the following: women; loss; hate; December 6; emotion; remembering; violence.

Directions:

Line 1: Give a one-word name, which is the subject of the stanza.
Line 2: Give two words to describe the first line.
Line 3: Follow this with three action words.
Line 4: Create a phrase descriptive of the subject.
Line 5: Summarize in one word.[4]

For example:
Stephanie
Bright star
Living, breathing, loving
The future unfolding
Gone

What I Know

The Canadian-born singer-songwriter Ferron tells a story about waking up one day during a gruelling performance tour and being completely lost—where was she? Why? *Who* was she? Upon becoming reoriented she rushed for a pen to write down everything she knew in case it should ever happen again. It seemed even more important to do now that she had a three-year-old daughter. Maybe one day *she'd* be lost on the road, and would need and welcome her mother's map.

What do *you* know? Imagine you have twenty minutes to write down everything you need to remember for yourself and share with those you most love. Write quickly; time is passing.

After you have recorded what you know, answer this: How can I use what I know in some initiative to combat violence against women?

Factsheet: Violence against Women and Girls

Selections from a fact sheet by Marika Morris, for the Canadian Research Institute for the Advancement of Women (CRIAW). Updated March 2002.

What is violence against women?

Violence can be physical (such as punching, kicking, choking, stabbing, mutilation, disabling, murder), sexual (such as rape, any unwanted touching or act of a sexual nature, forced prostitution), verbal/psychological (such as threats to harm the children, destruction of favourite clothes or photographs, repeated insults meant to demean and erode self-esteem, forced isolation from friends and relatives, threats of further violence or deportation if the woman attempts to leave), stalking (such as persistent and unwanted attention, following and spying, monitoring of mail or conversations), financial (such as taking away a woman's wages or other income, limiting or forbidding access to the family income), and other forms of control and abuse of power. Violence against women is about the control and coercion of women. It is a significant problem in Canada and around the world, also including female genital mutilation, child marriage, dowry-related murder, honour killings, female infanticide, and trafficking in women. Mass rapes and enslavement of women are also used as an instrument of war and genocide.

- Half of Canadian women have survived at least one incident of sexual or physical violence.

- Over a quarter (29%) of Canadian women have been assaulted by a spouse. Forty-five percent of women assaulted by a male partner suffered physical injury. Injuries included bruising, cuts, scratches, burns, broken bones, fractures, internal injuries, and miscarriages

- In Canada, four out of five people murdered by their spouses are women murdered by men. In 1998, 67 women were killed by a current or ex-spouse, boyfriend or ex-boyfriend. That's one to two women per week. In 6 out of 10 spousal murders, police were already aware that violence characterized the relationship

- Girl children are targets of abuse within the family more so than are boys. Four out of five victims of family-related sexual assaults (79%) are girls, and over half (55%) of physical assaults of children by family members are against girls. In 1997, fathers accounted for 97% of sexual assaults and 71% of physical assaults of children by parents

- Only 10% of sexual assaults on women are reported to the police. Extrapolating from these data, there are 509,860 reported and unreported sexual assaults in Canada per year. That's 1,397 per day; which means that every minute of every day, a woman or child in Canada is being sexually assaulted. Very often, sexual assaults are repeated on the same woman or child by the same offender.

- Ninety-eight percent of sex offenders are men and 82% of the survivors of these assaults are girls and women.

- Forty-three percent of women in one study reported at least one incident of unwanted sexual touching, forced or attempted forced sexual intercourse, or being forced to perform other acts of a sexual nature before the age of 16. The majority of these cases were at the level of unwanted sexual touching, usually repeated incidents by the same offender.

- Sexual assaults often occur in contexts in which the abuser is in a position of trust in relation to the person assaulted, such as a husband, father, other relative, doctor, coach, religious advisor, teacher, friend, employer, or date. The majority of sexual assaults are committed by a man known to the victim who is likely to use verbal pressure, tricks and/or threats during an assault. Two-thirds of sexual assaults occur in a private home.

- Wife battering carries on into old age. Spousal homicide accounts for one third (30%) of murders of women over 65.

- A minimum of one million Canadian children have witnessed violence against their mothers by their fathers or father figures. In 52% of these cases, the mother feared for her life, and in 61%, the mother sustained physical injuries. Children who witness violence against their mothers often exhibit signs of post-traumatic stress disorder, and their social skills and school achievement are adversely affected.

- Fear of violence also limits many women's lives. Forty-two percent of women compared with 10% of men feel "totally unsafe" walking in their own neighbourhood after dark, which in Canadian winters can begin at 3:30 PM, even earlier in the north. Over a third (37%) of women, compared with one in ten men, are worried about being in their own homes alone in the evening or night.

- In Canada, a man who beats and rapes his female partner can stay in his own home while the woman and children must sometimes move from shelter to shelter, disrupting their lives, work or schooling. In a 1993 survey, 295,000 abused Canadian women had no access to counselling or housing services.

Notes

Preface

1 Beverly Wildung Harrison, "Theological Reflection in the Struggle for Liberation," in *Making the Connections: Essays in Feminist Social Ethics,* ed. Carol S. Robb (Boston: Beacon Press, 1985), 236.

Introduction

1 Margaret Atwood, "Disembarking at Quebec" and "Further Arrivals," in Margaret Atwood, *Selected Poems* (Toronto: Oxford University Press, 1976), 80–81.

2 Susanna Moodie, *Roughing It in the Bush* (Toronto: McClelland and Stewart, 1923), 38.

3 Moodie, *Roughing It in the Bush,* 7.

4 Heather Murray, "Women in the Wilderness," in *A Mazing Space: Writing Canadian Women Writing,* ed. Shirley Neuman and Smaro Kamboureli (Edmonton: Longspoon/Newest, 1986), 75.

5 Peter Eglin and Stephen Hester, *The Montreal Massacre: A Story of Membership Categorization Analysis* (Waterloo, ON: Wilfrid Laurier University Press, 2003), 21.

6 "59% Call Massacre Only Random Act, Poll Finds." *Toronto Star,* December 29, 1989, A1, A4.

7 Pauline Greenhill, "A Good Start: A Graffiti Interpretation of the Montreal Massacre," *Atlantis* 17, no. 2 (Spring/Summer 1992): 108.

8 Dorothy E. Smith and Naomi Hersom, eds., *Women and the Canadian Labour Force* (Ottawa: Social Sciences and Humanities Research Council of Canada, 1982), 375.

9 I borrow here from Sharon Welch's reading of Adrienne Rich, who describes "feminist spirituality as 'casting one's lot' with those who resist, of continuing to affirm life in the midst of systematic denials of life." Sharon Welch, *Communities of Resistance and Solidarity: A Feminist Theology of Liberation* (Maryknoll, NY: Orbis, 1985), 8.

10 Elisabeth Schüssler Fiorenza, *In Memory of Her: A Feminist Theological Reconstruction of Christian Origins* (New York: Crossroads, 1983), xix.

11 Beverly Wildung Harrison, "Agendas for a New Theological Ethic," in *Churches in Struggle: Liberation Theologies and Social Change in North America*, ed. William Tabb (New York: Monthly Review Press, 1986), 93. Emphasis in original.

12 Welch, *Communities of Resistance and Solidarity*, 49.

13 Dorothy E. Smith, *The Everyday World as Problematic: A Feminist Sociology* (Toronto: University of Toronto Press, 1987), 157.

14 Dorothy E. Smith, *Feminism and Marxism: A Place to Begin and a Way to Go* (Vancouver: New Star Books, 1977), 9.

15 Smith and Hersom, *Women and the Canadian Labour Force*, 375.

16 Gregory Baum, "Faith and Liberation: Development since Vatican II," in Baum, *Theology and Society* (New York: Paulist Press, 1987), 5.

17 Gregory Baum, "The Impact of Sociology on Catholic Theology," in *Theology and Sociology: A Reader*, ed. Robin Gill (New York: Paulist Press, 1987), 138–39.

18 Smith, *The Everyday World*, 215.

19 Ibid., 142.

20 Gregory Baum, *Religion and Alienation: A Theological Reading of Sociology* (New York: Paulist Press, 1975), 193.

Chapter 1

1 Jerome H. Rosenberg, *Margaret Atwood* (Boston: Twayne, 1984), 41.

2 See Margaret Atwood, "The Planters" and "Dream 2: Brian the Still-Hunter," in *Selected Poems* (Toronto: Oxford University Press, 1976), 84 and 99, respectively.

3 Rosenberg, *Margaret Atwood*, 42.

4 Rosemary Radford Ruether, *Sexism and God-Talk: Toward a Feminist Theology* (Boston: Beacon Press, 1983), 187.

5 Gregory Baum, "Literary Praxis," *The Ecumenist* 25, no. 2 (May–June 1987): 60.

6 Gregory Baum, "Gutierrez and the Catholic Tradition," *The Ecumenist* 21, no. 6 (September–October 1983): 82. Baum describes here Gutierrez' position, but it is identical to his own.

7 Gregory Baum, "Three Theses on Contextual Theology," in Baum, *Theology and Society* (New York: Paulist Press, 1987), 168.

8 Gregory Baum, "A Response to Haight, Hutchinson, Simpson, and Rotstein," *Toronto Journal of Theology* 3, no. 2 (Fall 1987): 207.

9 Gregory Baum, "Personal Experience and Styles of Thought," in *Journeys: The Impact of Personal Experience on Religious Thought*, ed. Baum (New York: Paulist Press, 1975), 7.

10 Baum, "A Response," 204–205.

11 Gregory Baum, *Religion and Alienation: A Theological Reading of Sociology* (New York: Paulist Press, 1975), 1.

12 See Baum, "Personal Experience," 21.

13 Baum, "A Response," 204–205.

14 Gregory Baum, "Personal Testimony to Sociology," *The Ecumenist* 8, no. 1 (November–December 1969): 1. See Baum, "Remarks of a Theologian in Dialogue with Sociology," for an overview of Baum's introduction to and subsequent use of sociology in theology, and his critique of various sociological approaches to the study of religion. In *Theology and the Social Sciences*, ed. Michael Horace Barnes (Maryknoll, NY: Orbis, 2001), 3–11.

15 Timothy Radcliff, "A Theological Assessment of Sociological Explanation," in *Theology and Sociology: A Reader*, ed. Robin Gill (New York: Paulist Press, 1987), 167.

16 Dorothy E. Smith, *The Everyday World as Problematic: A Feminist Sociology* (Toronto: University of Toronto Press, 1987), 2.

17 Roger Haight, review of *Theology and Society*, by Gregory Baum, *Studies in Religion* 81, no. 1 (1989): 98.

18 Baum, "Three Theses," 157.

19 Ibid., 158.

20 Ibid., 160.

21 Baum, "Gutierrez and the Catholic Tradition," 82.

22 Sharon Welch, *Communities of Resistance and Solidarity: A Feminist Theology of Liberation* (Maryknoll, NY: Orbis, 1985), 28.

23 Baum, "Three Theses," 157.

24 Ibid., 160.

25 Ibid., 162.

26 Smith, *The Everyday World*, 154.

27 Gregory Baum, "Theological Methodology: The Magisterium," *The Ecumenist* 27, no. 5 (July–August 1989): 74.

28 Gregory Baum, "The Presence of the Church in Society," *Catholic Mind*, December 1970, 36.

29 Baum, "Gutierrez and the Catholic Tradition," 81.

30 Gregory Baum, "Theology in the Americas: Detroit II," *The Ecumenist* 18, no. 16 (September–October 1980): 91.

31 Gregory Baum, "Political Theology in Canada," *The Ecumenist* 15, no. 3 (March–April 1977): 34.

32 Ibid., 40.

33 Gregory Baum, "The Impact of Sociology on Catholic Theology," in *Theology and Sociology: A Reader*, ed. Gill, 138–39.

34 Paulo Freire, *Pedagogy of the Oppressed* (New York: Seabury Press, 1970), 66.

35 Baum, "Three Theses," 162.

36 Baum, "Humanistic Sociology, Scientific and Critical," in Baum, *Theology and Society*, 214.

37 Ibid., 227.

38 Ibid., 217.

39 Ibid., 227.

40 Baum, "Three Theses," 164.

41 Ibid., 167.

42 Ibid., 169.

43 Gregory Baum, "Afterword," in *Faith That Transforms: Essays in Honor of Gregory Baum*, ed. Mary Jo Leddy and Mary Ann Hinsdale (New York: Paulist Press, 1987), 140–41.

44 Ibid., 142–43.

45 Baum, *Compassion and Solidarity: The Church for Others*, CBC Massey Lecture Series (Toronto: CBC Enterprises, 1987), 30.

46 Gregory Baum, "Option for the Powerless," *The Ecumenist* 26, no. 1 (November–December 1987): 7.

47 Gregory Baum, "Toward a Canadian Catholic Social Theory," in Baum, *Theology and Society*, 72.

48 Brian Bergman, "Sisterhood of Fear and Fury," *Maclean's*, December 18, 1989, 18.

49 Baum, "Literary Praxis," 60.

50 Baum, "Three Theses," 170.

51 Ibid., 174.

52 Ibid., 172–74.

53 Ibid., 175.

54 Ibid., 176.

55 Baum, *Religion and Alienation*, 218–19.

56 Baum, "Three Theses," 176.

57 Baum, "Afterword," 145.

58 Margot Lacroix, "Slowing Down the Process of Forgetting," review of *The Montreal Massacre*, ed. Louise Malette and Marie Chalough, *Kinesis*, October 1991, 14.

59 Baum, "Three Theses," 57.

60 In "The Homosexual Condition and Political Responsibility," Baum writes that "the ambivalent position of belonging and not-belonging allows gay men and women to become perceptive critics of the social order. The comment is applicable also to women who are both part of and excluded from what Smith calls the relations of ruling. See Gregory Baum, "The Homosexual Condition and Political Responsibility," in *A Challenge to Love: Gay and Lesbian Catholics in the Church*, ed. Robert Nugent (New York: Crossroad, 1984), 39.

61 Gregory Baum, "Sociology and Salvation: Do We Need a Catholic Sociology?" *Theological Studies* 50, no. 4 (1989): 739.

62 Baum, "Remarks of a Theologian in Dialogue with Sociology," 9–10.

63 Dorothy E. Smith, *Texts, Facts, and Femininity: Exploring the Relations of Ruling* (New York: Routledge, 1990), 1.

64 Dorothy E. Smith and Alison Griffith, "Constructing Cultural Knowledge: Mothering as Discourse," in *Women and Education: A Canadian Perspective*, ed. Jane Gaskell and Arlene McLaren (Calgary: Detselig Enterprises, 1987), 88.

65 Smith, "Feminism and the Malepractice of Sociology," *Popular Feminism Papers* 3 (Toronto: Ontario Institute for Studies in Education, 1986): 2–3.

66 Smith, "The Malepractice of Sociology," 4–5.

67 Smith, *The Everyday World*, 2.

68 Ibid., 152.

69 Smith, *The Conceptual Practices of Power: A Feminist Sociology of Knowledge* (Boston: Northeastern University Press, 1990), 15.

70 Smith, *The Everyday World*, 152.

71 Smith, "The Malepractice of Sociology," 2–3.

72 Smith, *The Conceptual Practices of Power*, 200.

73 Smith, *The Conceptual Practices of Power*, 55.

74 Katherine Cook, "Women's Sociology" (M.A. thesis, Toronto: Ontario Institute for Studies in Education, 1981), 20.

75 Smith, *The Conceptual Practices of Power*, 4.

76 "University Fights Outbreak of Sexism Virus," *Globe and Mail*, April 25, 1990, A1–2.

77 Dorothy E. Smith, "Women and Psychiatry," in *Women Look at Psychiatry*, ed. Dorothy E. Smith and Sarah Davids (Vancouver: Press Gang, 1975), 366.

78 Dorothy E. Smith, "Women's Perspective as a Radical Critique of Sociology," *Sociological Inquiry* 44, no. 1 (1974): 7.

79 Smith, *The Conceptual Practices of Power*, 199.

80 Ibid., 12.

81 Smith, *The Everyday World*, 107.

82 Smith, "The Malepractice of Sociology," 5.

83 Smith and Griffith, "Constructing Cultural Knowledge," 90. Emphasis in original.

84 Smith, "The Malepractice of Sociology," 8.

85 Smith, "Feminist Reflections on Political Economy," *Studies in Political Economy* 30 (Autumn 1989): 39.

86 Dorothy E. Smith, "Women, Class and Family," in *Women, Class, Family and the State*, ed. Varda Burstyn and Dorothy E. Smith (Toronto: Garamond, 1985), 3.

87 Dorothy E. Smith, "Institutional Ethnography: A Feminist Method," *Gender and Society: Creating a Canadian Women's Sociology*, ed. Arlene Tigar McLaren (Toronto: Copp Clark Pitman, 1988), 63.

88 Dorothy E. Smith, "Sociological Theory: Methods of Writing Patriarchy," in *Feminism and Sociological Theory*, ed. Ruth A. Wallace (Newbury Park, CA: Sage, 1989), 37.

89 Dorothy E. Smith, "A Sociology for Women," in *The Prism of Sex: Essays in the Sociology of Knowledge*, ed. Julia A. Sherman and Evelyn T. Beck (Madison, WI: University of Wisconsin Press, 1979), 170.

90 Smith, "A Sociology for Women," 170.

91 Smith, *The Everyday World*, 110.

92 Ibid., 99.

93 Ibid., 148.

94 Dorothy E. Smith, "On Sociological Description: A Method from Marx," *Human Studies* 4 (1981): 316.

95 Naomi Hersom and Dorothy E. Smith, *Women and the Canadian Labour Force* (Ottawa: Social Sciences and Humanities Research Council of Canada, 1982), 375.

96 Smith, *The Everyday World*, 134.

97 Ibid., 157.

98 Ibid., 154.

99 Smith, "The Malepractice of Sociology," 7.

100 Meg Luxton and Sue Findlay, "Is the Everyday World the Problematic? Reflections on Smith's Method of Making Sense of Experience," *Studies in Political Economy* 30 (Autumn 1989): 185.

101 Kathleen Storrie, "The Everyday World as Problematic: A Bridge between the Academy and the University," in *From the Margins to the Centre: Essays in Women's Studies Research*, ed. Dawn Currie (Saskatoon, SK: Women's Studies Research Unit, 1988), 127.

102 Beverly Wildung Harrison, "The Role of Social Theory in Religious Social Ethics," in *Making the Connections: Essays in Feminist Social Ethics*, ed. Carol S. Robb (Boston: Beacon Press, 1985), 79.

103 Dorothy E. Smith, "What It Might Mean to Do a Canadian Sociology: The Everyday World as Problematic," *Canadian Journal of Sociology* 1, no. 3 (Fall 1975): 374.

104 Smith, "Feminist Reflections on Political Economy," 41.

105   Dorothy E. Smith, "Editor's Introduction: On Sally Hacker's Method," in Hacker, *Doing It the Hard Way: Investigations of Gender and Technology*, ed. Dorothy Smith and Susan Turner (Boston: Unwin Hyman, 1990), 3.

106   Smith, "Institutional Ethnography," 66.

107   Dorothy E. Smith, "The Social Organization of Knowledge" (course outline, Ontario Institute for Studies in Education, Fall, 1988), 1.

108   Smith, *The Conceptual Practices of Power*, 4.

109   Smith, "The Social Organization of Knowledge," 2.

110   Gillian Walker, *Family Violence and the Women's Movement* (Toronto: University of Toronto Press, 1990), 10.

111   Smith, *The Everyday World*, 122.

112   Gregory Baum, "Foreword," in Baum, *Theology and Society*, v.

113   Smith, "The Malepractice of Sociology," 7.

114   Dorothy E. Smith, "Some Implications of a Sociology for Women," in *Woman in a Man-Made World: A Socio-economic Handbook*, ed. Nona Glazer and Helen Waehrer (Chicago: Rand-McNally, 1977), 21.

115   Dorothy E. Smith, *Feminism and Marxism: A Place to Begin and a Way to Go* (Vancouver: New Star Books, 1977), 12.

116   Baum, "Humanistic Sociology," 214.

117   Smith, *Feminism and Marxism*, 12. According to Baum, a sociological approach should uncover the structures and attitudes of domination and bring to consciousness the subjectivity of the researcher if it is to be adequate theologically. Baum, "Humanistic Sociology," 227.

118   Baum, "Humanistic Sociology," 217.

119   Maria Mies, "Towards a Methodology for Feminist Research," in *Theories of Women's Studies*, ed. Gloria Bowles and Renate Duelli Klein (Boston: Routledge and Kegan Paul, 1983), 124. Baum would most certainly agree.

120   Baum, "Humanistic Sociology," 227.

121   Baum, "Three Theses," 162.

122   Smith, "What It Might Mean," 365.

123   Smith, "Some Implications of a Sociology for Women," 26.

124   Baum, "Three Theses," 170.

125   Smith, *The Everyday World*, 106.

126   Sandra Harding, "Is There a Feminist Method?" in Harding (Bloomington, IN: Indiana University Press, 1987), 5.

127   Baum, *Religion and Alienation*, 258.

128   Leslie Miller, review of *The Everyday World as Problematic* by Dorothy E. Smith, *The Canadian Journal of Sociology* 14, no. 4 (Fall 1989): 523.

129   Gregory Baum, "The Creed That Liberates," *Horizons* 13, no. 1 (Spring 1986): 142.

130   Baum, "Three Theses," 157.

Chapter 2

1   *Maclean's*, December 18, 1989.

2   "Funds Reduced or Ended for Outspoken Women's, Native Groups," *Globe and Mail*, February 23, 1990, A13.

3   Dorothy E. Smith, *The Everyday World as Problematic: A Feminist Sociology* (Toronto: University of Toronto Press, 1987), 154.

4   Smith, *The Everyday World*, 9.

5   John Simpson, "Gregory Baum and Sociology," *Toronto Journal of Theology* 3, no. 2 (Fall 1987): 195.

6   Special Issue. Canada's Century: The 25 Events That Shaped the Country. *Maclean's*, July 1, 1999.

7   Sylvie Gagnon, interviewed in *After the Montreal Massacre* (Toronto: Studio D, National Film Board, 1990).

8   See for instance Lee Lakeman, "Women, Violence and the Montreal Massacre," *This Magazine* 23, no. 7 (March 1990), and Louise Malette, "Letter to the Media," in *The Montreal Massacre*, ed. Louise Malette and Marie Chalouh, trans. Marlene Wildeman (Charlottetown, PE: gynergy, 1991), 56–57.

9   Smith, *The Everyday World*, 50.

10 See Armande Saint-Jean, "Burying Women's Words: An Analysis of Media Attitudes," in *The Montreal Massacre*, 62–63.

11 Dorothy E. Smith, *The Conceptual Practices of Power: A Feminist Sociology of Knowledge* (Toronto: University of Toronto Press, 1990), 28.

12 Smith, *The Conceptual Practices of Power*, 200, 206.

13 Smith, *The Everyday World*, 212.

14 Dorothy E. Smith, *Texts, Facts, and Femininity: Exploring the Relations of Ruling* (New York: Routledge, 1990), 164.

15 Dorothy E. Smith, "The Deep Structure of Gender Antithesis: Another View of Capitalism and Patriarchy," in *A Feminist Ethic for Social Science Research*, Nebraska Sociological Feminist Collective (Leviston, NY: Edwin Mellen Press, 1988), 23.

16 Dorothy E. Smith, "An Analysis of Ideological Structures and How Women Are Excluded: Considerations for Academic Women," *Canadian Review of Sociology and Anthropology* 12, no. 4 (1975): 355.

17 *After the Montreal Massacre*, National Film Board, Studio D.

18 Ursula Franklin, "Community and Technology," *Canadian Forum* 791 (July–August 1990): 22.

19 Smith, "An Analysis of Ideological Structures," 356.

20 Smith, *The Conceptual Practices of Power*, 83.

21 Dorothy E. Smith, "Textually Mediated Social Organization," *International Social Science Journal* 366, no. 1 (1984): 65.

22 Dorothy E. Smith, "On Sociological Description: A Method from Marx," *Human Studies* 4 (1981): 313.

23 I focus primarily but not exclusively here on the printed media, primarily but not exclusively on the time period between the 6th and the end of December, 1989. References are made to the *Globe and Mail* (Toronto), for that time period, to the *Gazette* (Montreal), December 7 and 12, and to other papers referred to by commentators on the media presentation. The choice of the *Globe and Mail* and the *Gazette* as points of departure from which to present the coverage of the massacre is an arbitrary one; I happen to have these papers with me as I write. They are referred to not as a case study but as a place from which to comment on the portrayal and characterization of the massacre in the mainstream press. My reading of commentaries on the presentations of other newspapers suggests that these were not atypical in their approaches. It should be noted that while the choice of papers is arbitrary, it is not insignificant. The *Globe and Mail* is Canada's national newspaper, and the massacre occurred in Montreal, home of the *Gazette*.

24 François Bordeleau and Robert Labelle, respectively, quoted in Peter Kuiten-brouwer, Marian Scott, Mary Lamey, and Jeff Heinrich, "Gunman Kills 14 Women before Shooting Himself," *Gazette*, December 7, 1989, A1–2.

25 Mayor Jean Doré and Director Roland Doré, respectively, quoted in Kuiten-brouwer, Scott, Lamey, and Heinrich, "Gunman Kills 14 Women before Shoot-ing Himself," *Gazette*, December 7, 1989, A1–2.

26 Kuitenbrouwer, Scott, Lamey, and Heinrich, "Gunman Kills 14 Women before Shooting Himself," *Gazette*, December 7, 1989, A1–2.

27 Julien Feldman, "University Massacre Was Nation's Worst," *Gazette*, Decem-ber 7, 1989, A4.

28 Gazette Staff, "Politicians Express Shock, Sympathy as Assembly Stops Education Debate," *Gazette*, December 7, 1989, A3.

29 *Globe and Mail*, December 7, 1989, A1, A5.

30 Myriame El Yamani, "La mascarade médiatique," *Sociologie et Sociétés* 22, no. 1 (April 1990): 203. [Narration, as journalists use it ... allows them to describe without having to explain, to create a story while hiding the social, historical, and political context in which the event took place. The only elements of context that the six daily papers under consideration will publish will be a wire-service dispatch providing a retrospective, through time and around the world, of this type of serial slaughter. —My translation]

31 As described by Melanie Randall, "Men Cannot Know the Feelings of Fear," *Globe and Mail*, December 12, 1989, A7.

32 El Yamani, "La mascarade médiatique," 203. [December 8: the media continue to produce a slew of ephemeral stories that make the whole affair seem like an uncontrollable series of events and above all one that does not permit any doubt or questioning of its presentation. So here we enter into the strategy of intense emphasis on psychology.... It's at just this moment that every imaginable sort of expert arrives on the scene: psychologists, psychiatrists, doctors, priests, legal experts, police officers,... etc. —My translation]

33 See Marie-Andrée Bertrand, "Analyse criminologique d'un meurtre commis dans l'enceinte de l'université et des interprétations que certains groupes choisissent d'en donner," *Sociologie et Sociétés* 22, no. 1 (April 1990): 195–96.

34 Patricia Poirier and Barrie McKenna, "Quebec Mourns Slaying of Women at University," *Globe and Mail*, December 8, 1989, A1, A14.

35 See the *Globe and Mail*, December 8, 1989: "Why Were Women in the Gunsight?" A6; Emil Sher, "Speaking about the Unspeakable," A7; Diana Bronson, "A Time for Grief and Pain," A7.

36 Michele Landsberg, "Killer's Rage Too Familiar to Canadians," *Toronto Star*, December 8, 1989, A1, A16.

37 Lakeman, "Women, Violence and the Montreal Massacre," 21–22.

38 See the *Globe and Mail*, December 9, 1989: Benoit Aubin, "Don't Have Feelings of Guilt, Woman Hurt in Massacre Urges Her Fellow Students," A1, A2; Victor Malarek, "Killer Fraternized with Men in Army Fatigues," A5; "The Semi-Auto-matic Response," D6; John Allemang, "Violence and Anger," D6; and Stevie Cameron, "Our Daughters, Ourselves," D1, D8.

39 Joan Baril, "At the Centre of the Backlash," *Canadian Forum* 786 (February 1990): 14, 16–17.

40 "Letter to the Editor," *Globe and Mail*, December 21, 1989, A6.

41 Baril, "At the Centre of the Backlash," 16.

42 Debbie Wise Harris, "Keeping Women in Our Place," *Canadian Woman Studies* 11, no. 4 (Summer 1991): 41.

43 "Ordinary Folks Share Grief in Vigil by Church," *Gazette*, December 12, 1989, A7. The first four pages of the *Gazette* that day were taken up with the stories mentioned.

44 El Yamani, "La mascarade médiatique," 203. [Who would not be … moved by the sight … of the father of one of the victims bursting into tears in front of the coffin of his daughter?… This journalistic technique does not happen by chance; on the contrary, it has the goal of reducing the incomprehensibility of society and reinforcing the concept of a coherent society. —My translation]

45 Sylvie Bérard, "Words and Deeds," in *The Montreal Massacre*, 77.

46 See "59% Call Massacre Only Random Act, Poll Finds," *Toronto Star*, December 29, 1989, A1, A4.

47 Jane Caputi and Diana Russell, "'Femicide': Speaking the Unspeakable," *Ms.*, September–October 1990, 35.

48 Ruth Roach Pierson, "Violence against Women: Strategies for Change," *Canadian Woman Studies* 11, no. 4 (Summer 1991): 11.

49 Saint-Jean, "Burying Women's Words," 62.

50 Louise Bonnier, "Genealogy," in *The Montreal Massacre*, 153.

51 See Dorothy E. Smith and Naomi Hersom, *Women and the Canadian Labour Force* (Ottawa: Social Sciences and Humanities Research Council of Canada, 1982), 270.

52 Smith, *The Conceptual Practices of Power*, 83.

53 Lisa Schmidt, "Sorrow, Anger after Montreal," *Kinesis*, February 1990, 7.

54 Pauline Greenhill, "A Good Start: A Graffiti Interpretation of the Montreal Massacre," *Atlantis* 17, no. 2: 109.

55 Rudy Kafer, Barbara Hodkin, David Furrow, and Trudy Landry, "What Do the Montreal Murders Mean? Attitudinal and Demographic Predictors of Attribution," *Canadian Journal of Behavioural Science* 25, no. 4 (October 1993): 543.

56 Maureen Bradley, *Reframing the Montreal Massacre: A Media Interrogation* (Vancouver: Mediawise, 1995).

57 Smith, *The Everyday World*, 57.

58 Ibid., *The Everyday World*, 56.

59 Dorothy E. Smith, "Sociological Theory: Methods of Writing Patriarchy," in *Feminism and Sociological Theory*, ed. Ruth Wallace (Newbury Park, CA: Sage, 1989), 38.

60 Women are discounted speakers in public discourse. See Smith, *The Conceptual Practices of Power*, 101–103, for Smith's elaboration of this.

61 Lorraine Code, "Credibility: A Double Standard," in *Feminist Perspectives: Philosophical Essays on Method and Morals*, ed. Lorraine Code, Sheila Mullett, and Christine Overall (Toronto: University of Toronto Press, 1988), 64.

62 Smith, "Ideological Structures," 358.

63 Smith, *The Everyday World*, 220.

64 Rose Sheinin, "La Suite du 6 Décembre," in "Women in Scholarship: One Step Forward, Two Steps Back?" *Royal Society of Canada Proceedings* (University of Victoria, BC, June 3, 1990), 3.

65 Gillian Walker, *Family Violence and the Women's Movement* (Toronto: University of Toronto Press, 1990), 9.

66 Vaughn Jelliffe, "How PEI Women's Groups Responded to the Murder of 14 Students in Montreal," *Common Ground* 9, no. 1 (February 1990): 8.

67 Lakeman, "Women, Violence and the Montreal Massacre," 22.

68 Maria de Koninck and Diane Lamoureux, "That They Not Be Forgotten...," in *The Montreal Massacre*, 118.

69 Andrea Dworkin, "Terror, Torture and Resistance," *Canadian Woman Studies* 12, no. 1 (Fall 1991): 40.

70 Walker, *Family Violence and the Women's Movement*, 215.

71 See Dorothy E. Smith, "Women's Perspective as a Radical Critique of Sociology," *Sociological Inquiry* 4, no. 1 (1974): 7.

72 Caputi and Russell, "Femicide," 34, 36.

73 Elaine Audet, "A Matter of Life or Death," in *The Montreal Massacre*, 44.

74 Margot Lacroix, "Slowing Down the Process of Forgetting," review of *The Montreal Massacre, Kinesis*, October 1991, 14.

75 Alanna Mitchell, "Montreal Massacre a Catalyst for Action," *Globe and Mail*, December 3, 1991, A1.

76 Dorothy E. Smith, "The Statistics on Mental Illness: What They Will Not Tell Us about Women and Why," in *Women Look at Psychiatry*, ed. Dorothy Smith and Sarah Davids (Vancouver: Press Gang, 1975), 97.

77 Smith, *The Everyday World*, 56.

78 Patricia Poirier, "Slain Woman's Connection to Killer Called Just Coincidence by Police," *Globe and Mail*, December 12, 1989, A12.

79 "Inquest Is Unlikely—Coroner," *Gazette*, December 12, 1989, A5.

80 Smith, *The Conceptual Practices of Power*," 144.

81 Dorothy E. Smith, "K Is Mentally Ill: The Anatomy of a Factual Account," *Sociology* 12, no. 1 (1978): 24.

82 Smith, *The Conceptual Practices of Power*, 160.

83 Smith, *The Everyday World*, 162.

84 Smith, *The Conceptual Practices of Power*, 93–94.

85 Smith, *The Everyday World*, 162.

86 Smith, *The Conceptual Practices of Power*, 93–94.

87 Victor Malarek and Benoit Aubin, "Killer's Letter Blames Feminists," *Globe and Mail*, December 8, 1989, A1.

88 Victor Malarek, "Police Refusal to Answer Questions Leaves Lots of Loose Ends in Killings," *Globe and Mail*, December 13, 1989, A8.

89 Patricia Poirier, "Lépine Could Have Shot Many Others, Coroner Says," *Globe and Mail*, May 15, 1990, A1, A2.

90 Smith, *The Conceptual Practices of Power*, 94.

91 Walker, *Family Violence and the Women's Movement*, 13, 148.

92 Patricia Poirier, "Quebec Assailed for Not Improving Emergency Teams," *Globe and Mail*, March 28, 1991, A4.

93 Walker, *Family Violence and the Women's Movement*, 100–101. Walker's study focuses on battered women, whom she refers to here. Her point is equally applicable to this situation.

94 Alanna Mitchell, "Montreal Massacre a Catalyst for Action," *Globe and Mail*, December 3, 1991, A1, A10.

95 Glen Allen, "In the Cross Hairs," *Maclean's*, May 6, 1991, 26.

96 Ibid., 26.

97 David Vienneau, "New Gun Law said 'Tribute' to 14 Victims," *Toronto Star*, December 6, 1991, A1.

98 Bruce Wallace, "The Minister Takes Aim," *Maclean's*, June 3, 1991, 12.

99 Vienneau, "New Gun Law Said 'Tribute,'" *Toronto Star*, December 6, 1991, A1.

100 Canadian Broadcasting Corporation, December 6, 1990.

101 André Picard, "Victims' Families Express Anger over Non-voice," *Globe and Mail*, January 12, 1991, A5.

102 Dorothy E. Smith, "Gender, Power and Peace," in *Up and Doing: Canadian Women and Peace*, ed. Janice Williamson and Deborah Gorham (Toronto: Women's Press, 1989), 99–100.

103 Thomas Gabor, "The Federal Gun Registry: An Urgent Need for Independent, Non-partisan Research," *Canadian Journal of Criminology and Criminal Justice* 45, no. 4 (Oct. 2003): 490.

104 Standing Committee on Health and Welfare, Social Affairs, Seniors and the Status of Women, *The War against Women* (Ottawa: June 1991), 3.

105 Penni Mitchell, "What Has to Happen to Stop the Violence?" *Herizons*, Spring 1992, 17.

106 "Government Supports Report on Violence against Women," *Globe and Mail*, November 8, 1991, A5.

107 Marika Morris, "Factsheet: Violence against Women and Girls," Canadian Research Institute for the Advancement of Women, 2002. http://www.criaw-icref .ca/factSheets/Violence_fact_sheet_e.htm (accessed June 28, 2004).

108 Marie-Claire Lévesque, "The Panel on Violence against Women," *Canadian Woman Studies* 12, no. 1 (Fall 1991): 118.

109 André Picard and Michelle LaLonde, "System Blamed for Recent Spate of Murder Cases," *Globe and Mail*, September 28, 1990, A8.

110 "Funds Reduced or Ended for Outspoken Women's, Native Groups," *Globe and Mail*, February 23, 1990, A13.

111 Smith, *The Conceptual Practices of Power*, 65.

112 Status of Women Canada, "Fry Announces Declaration of the Federal–Provincial/Territorial Status of Women Ministers on Violence against Women." http://www.swc-cfc.gc.ca/news98/1203-e.html (accessed January 10, 1999).

113 Status of Women Canada, "Violence against Women Continues to Be Problem: Serious Impacts on Canada's Health, Justice and Social System." http://www .swc-cfc.gc.ca/newsroom/news2002/1203_e.html (accessed July 15, 2004).

114 Valerie Lawton, "Canada Failing Its Women, U.N. Says." *Toronto Star*, March 6, 2003, A1.

115 Walker, *Family Violence and the Women's Movement*, 150.

116 Ibid., 106–107.

117 Graham Fraser, "Changing Men's Attitudes a Major Challenge, Collins Says," *Globe and Mail*, December 5, 1990.

118 Ailbhe Smyth, "Seeing Red: Men's Violence against Women in Ireland," in *Women in a Violent World: Feminist Analyses and Resistance across "Europe,"* ed. Chris Corrin (Edinburgh University Press, 1996), 69.

119 Dorothy Smith, "Where There Is Oppression There Is Resistance," *Branching Out* 6, no. 1 (1979): 13–14.

120 Ibid., 13–14.

121 See Patricia Morgan, "From Battered Wife to Program Client: The State's Shaping of Social Problems," *Kapitalistate* 9 (1981): 20.

122 Michael Kaufman, "Ten Years after the Montreal Massacre: The Terrible Moment That Brings Hope to the World." http://www.europrofem.org/06.actio/wrc_rib/erwc_en/07wrc_en.htm (accessed August 12, 2000).

123 Judy Rebick, "1989–Montreal Massacre," CBC News Online. wysiwyg://6/http://cbc.ca/millennium/timelines/feature_montreal.htm (accessed December 1, 2000).

124 *Globe and Mail* editorial, December 6, 1999, A16.

125 Ministry of Women's Equality, British Columbia, http://www.weq.gov.bc.ca/dec6/index.html (accessed June 18, 2000).

126 See, for example, Elizabeth Thompson, "Tragedy Touched Us All," *Gazette*, December 7, 2004.

127 Mitchell, "Montreal Massacre a Catalyst for Action," *Globe and Mail*, December 3, 1991, A1.

128 *The Concise Oxford Dictionary*, 7th ed., s.v. "real."

129 See Nancy Adamson, Linda Briskin, and Margaret Mcphail, *Feminist Organizing for Change: The Contemporary Women's Movement in Canada* (Toronto: Oxford University Press, 1988), 6.

130 Harris, "Keeping Women in Our Place," 37.

131 Morris, "Factsheet: Violence against Women and Girls."

132 Smith, *The Everyday World*, 25.

133 Ibid., 24–25.

134 Ibid., 54.

135 Smith, "Textually Mediated Social Organization," 63.

136 Smith, *Feminism and Marxism*, 18.

137 Smith, *The Conceptual Practices of Power*, 65. Smith refers here to boundaries set by the textual realities of the relations of ruling. I have expanded the reference.

Chapter 3

1 Janice Williamson, "'The Landscape from How I See My Poems Moving,' an interview with Bronwen Wallace," in *Open Letter*, 26–27. Wallace refers here to her 1987 book of poetry by that name. Bronwen Wallace, *The Stubborn Particulars of Grace* (Toronto: McClelland and Stewart, 1987).

2 Gregory Baum, "Afterword," in *Faith That Transforms: Essays in Honor of Gregory Baum*, ed. Mary Jo Leddy and Mary Ann Hinsdale (New York: Paulist Press, 1987), 139.

3 Gregory Baum, "God's Word as Judgement and New Life," *Chelsea Journal* 3, no. 3 (May–June 1977): 150.

4 Veronica Schild, "The Eclipse of Criticalness in Marxist Social Science: Habermas and Smith," M.A. thesis (Toronto: Ontario Institute for Studies in Education, 1982), 54.

5 Carter Heyward, "The Power of God-with-Us," *Christian Century* 107, no. 1 (March 14, 1990): 277.

6 Gregory Baum, "The Impact of Sociology on Catholic Theology," in *Theology and Sociology: A Reader*, ed. Robin Gill (New York: Paulist Press, 1987), 138–39.

7 Gregory Baum, "Literary Praxis," *The Ecumenist* 25, no. 2 (May–June 1987): 60.

8   Ibid.

9   John Simpson, "Gregory Baum and Sociology," *Toronto Journal of Theology* 3, no. 2 (Fall 1987): 195.

10 Jane Caputi and Diana Russell, "'Femicide': Speaking the Unspeakable," *Ms*, September–October 1990, 34.

11 Debbie Wise Harris, "Keeping Women in Our Place: Violence at Canadian Universities," *Canadian Woman Studies* 11, no. 4 (Summer 1991): 39.

12 Elaine Audet, "A Matter of Life or Death," in *The Montreal Massacre*, ed. Louise Malette and Marie Chalouh, trans. Marlene Wildeman (Charlottetown: gynergy books, 1991), 44.

13 Michael Valpy, "Litany of Social Ills Created Marc Lépine," *Globe and Mail*, December 11, 1989, A8.

14 Mary Daly, *Beyond God the Father*, cited in Sharon Welch, *Communities of Resistance and Solidarity: A Feminist Theology of Liberation* (Maryknoll, NY: Orbis, 1985), 48–49.

15 Gillian Walker, *Family Violence and the Women's Movement* (Toronto: University of Toronto Press, 1990), 215.

16 Nicholas Lash, *A Matter of Hope* (Notre Dame, IN: University of Notre Dame Press, 1981), 189.

17 Dorothy E. Smith, *The Conceptual Practices of Power: A Feminist Sociology of Knowledge* (Toronto: University of Toronto Press, 1990), 43.

18 Dorothy E. Smith, "The Ideological Practice of Sociology," *Catalyst* 8 (Winter 1974): 40. Italics in original.

19 Margot Lacroix, "The Montreal Massacre: Slowing Down the Process of Forgetting," review of *The Montreal Massacre*, in *Kinesis* (October 1991): 14.

20 Malette and Chalouh, eds., *The Montreal Massacre*, 59.

21 Ibid., 36.

22 "The Montreal Massacre: 14 Not Forgotten," *Imprint* 18, no. 19 (University of Waterloo, November 24, 1995). http://imprint.uwaterloo.ca/issues/112495/2Forum/fo7.html (accessed July 15, 2004).

23 Dorothy E. Smith, "Women and Psychiatry," in *Women Look at Psychiatry*, ed. Dorothy E. Smith and Sarah Davids (Vancouver: Press Gang, 1975), 13–14.

24 Ivor Shapiro, "Why Did Marc Lépine Murder 14 Women?" *Chatelaine*, June 1990, 76.

25 Louis Courville, "J'étais Là," in "Women in Scholarship: One Step Forward, Two Steps Back?" *Royal Society of Canada Proceedings* (University of Victoria, June 3, 1990), 2.

26 Dorothy E. Smith, *The Everyday World as Problematic: A Feminist Sociology* (Toronto: University of Toronto Press, 1987), 72–73.

27 Ibid., 71.

28 Beverly Wildung Harrison, *Making the Connections: Essays in Feminist Social Ethics*, ed. Carol S. Robb (Boston: Beacon Press, 1985), 14.

29 Smith, *The Conceptual Practices of Power*, 137.

30 Dorothy E. Smith, "Where There Is Oppression, There Is Resistance," *Branching Out* 6, no. 1 (1979): 13.

31 Freed, "Soul Searching in Montreal and Canada," *Canadian Dimension* 24, no. 2 (March 1990): 17.

32   "Government Supports Report on Violence against Women," *Globe and Mail*, November 8, 1991, A5.

33   Sharon Rosenberg, "Reflections on Memorializing December 6." *Resources for Feminist Research* 26, nos. 3–4 (Fall/Winter 1998/99): 207.

34   Fiona McQuarrie, "Letter to the Editor," *This Magazine*, August 1990, 10.

35   Smith, *The Conceptual Practices of Power*, 41.

36   Ibid., 42.

37   Walker, *Family Violence and the Women's Movement*, 85.

38   George Bain, "An Orgy over Whether All Men Are Vile," *Maclean's*, December 23, 1991, 48.

39   Henry Gale, "Not Collective Guilt, but Collective Responsibility," *Globe and Mail*, November 23, 1994, A24.

40   Rose Simone, "Feminism in the Media and the '90's Backlash." http://watserv1 .uwaterloo.ca/~facassoc/simone.html (accessed July 7, 2002).

41   Radical Lesbian Group, "Insignificant Violence?" *Connexions* 34 (1990), 8.

42   Catherine Nelson-McDermott, "Murderous Fallout: Post-Lépine Rhethoric." *Atlantis* 17, no. 1 (Fall/Winter 1991): 124–25.

43   Nicole Brossard, "One Year After," *This Magazine*, December–January 1991, 18.

44   Rose Marie Kennedy, "Remembering Montreal: For a Future without Fear," *Kinesis*, December/January 1992, 9.

45   Susan Rudy Dorscht, "Writing at the Interval," *Open Letter* 7, no. 9 (Winter 1991): 103.

46   Gregory Baum, "The Contemporary Social Gospel," *Proceedings of the 1978 Conference of the Institute for Christian Life in Canada* (Toronto: Institute for Christian Life in Canada, 1978).

47   Marcia Westkott, "Women's Studies as a Strategy for Change," in *Theories of Women's Studies*, ed. Gloria Bowles and Renata Duelli Klein (New York: Routledge & Kegan Paul, 1983), 216–17.

48   Baum, "Literary Praxis," 60.

49   Dorscht, "Writing at the Interval," 103.

50   Gregory Baum, "The Power of the Poor: Theological and Sociological Perspectives," *Catholic Theological Society of America Proceedings* 37 (1982), 168.

51   Margot Lettner, "One Year After," *This Magazine*, 23.

52   Harris, "Keeping Women in Our Place," 39.

53   Charlotte Bunch, in Nicole Hubert (producer), *After the Montreal Massacre* (Toronto: National Film Board, Studio D, 1990).

54   Caputi and Russell, "'Femicide': Speaking the Unspeakable," 37.

55   Catharine A. MacKinnon, *Feminism Unmodified*, cited in Bettina Aptheker, *Tapestries of Life: Women's Work, Women's Consciousness, and the Meaning of Daily Experience* (Amherst, MA: University of Massachusetts Press, 1989), 253.

56   Lori Haskell and Melanie Randall, "The Politics of Women's Safety: Sexual Violence, Women's Fear and the Public/Private Split." *Resources for Feminist Research* 26, nos. 3–4 (Fall/Winter 1998/99): 118.

57   Rosemary Gartner, Myrna Dawson, and Maria Crawford, "Woman Killing: Intimate Femicide in Ontario, 1974–1994." *Resources for Feminist Research* 26, nos. 3–4 (Fall/Winter 1998/99): 166–67.

58   Gregory Baum, *Essays in Critical Theology* (Kansas City: Sheed and Ward, 1994), 191–92.

59 The four levels are described in Gregory Baum, *Religion and Alienation: A Theological Reading of Sociology* (New York: Paulist Press, 1975), 201–202.

60 Monique Frize, "The Bold and the Brave: Women Engineers Striving for Change." CD-ROM, Proceedings of the ICWES12 Conference, Ottawa, July 2002, 4.

61 See Maureen Bradley's film, *Reframing the Montreal Massacre: A Media Interrogation* (Vancouver: Mediawise, 1995).

62 "Pay Equity," *Maclean's*, November 8, 2004, 15.

63 Baum, *Religion and Alienation*, 197.

64 Nicole Brossard in *The Montreal Massacre*, 33.

65 Baum, "Literary Praxis," 60.

66 Bronwen Wallace, "To Get to You," *Common Magic* (Toronto: Oberon Press, 1985), 56.

67 Gregory Baum, "Faith and Liberation: Development since Vatican II," in Baum, *Theology and Society* (New York: Paulist Press, 1987), 20.

68 Walker, *Family Violence and the Women's Movement*, 9.

69 Dorscht, "Writing at the Interval," 103.

70 James Mennie and Hubert Bauch, "A Quiet Goodbye for Slain Women," *Gazette*, December 12, 1989: A1.

71 Lash, *A Matter of Hope*, 193.

72 Gregory Baum, "Middle Class Religion in America," in *Christianity and the Bourgeoisie, Concilium 125*, ed. Johannes Baptist Metz (Edinburgh: T. & T. Clark, 1979), 21.

73 Andrea Dworkin, "Terror, Torture and Resistance," *Canadian Woman Studies* 12, no. 1 (Fall 1991): 41.

74 Mennie and Bauch, "A Quiet Goodbye for Slain Women."

75 Cardinal Paul-Emile Léger, December 8, 1989, CKAC Radio, cited in Côté, "The Art of Making It Work for You," in *The Montreal Massacre*, 67.

76 Baum, *Religion and Alienation*, 292.

77 Gregory Baum, *Truth beyond Relativism: Karl Mannheim's Sociology of Knowledge* (Milwaukee, WI: Marquette University Press, 1977), 75–76.

78 Harrison, *Making the Connections*, 263.

Chapter 4

1 Stevie Cameron, "Our Daughters, Ourselves," *Globe and Mail*, December 9, 1989, D1, D8.

2 Anne Tyler, "Still Just Writing," in *The Writer on Her Work: Contemporary Women Writers Reflect on Their Art and Situation*, ed. Janet Steinberg (New York: W.W. Norton, 1980), 15.

3 Beverly Wildung Harrison, "Theological Reflection in the Struggle for Liberation," in Harrison, *Making the Connections: Essays in Feminist Social Ethics*, ed. Carol S. Robb (Boston: Beacon Press, 1985), 249.

4 Wendy Hui Kyong Chun, "Unbearable Witness: Toward a Politics of Listening," *differences: A Journal of Feminist Cultural Studies* 11, no. 1 (1999): 113.

5 Jean F. O'Barr, "Identifying Sources of Resistance," in *Women Imagine Change: A Global Anthology of Women's Resistance from 600 B.C.E. to Present*, ed. Eugenia C. Delamotte, Natania Meeker, and Jean F. O'Barr (New York: Routledge, 1997), 298.

6 Randy Fabi, "Abuse Damages Health of One in Three Women: Study," *Globe and Mail*, January 21, 2000, A8.

7   bell hooks, *Talking Back: Thinking Feminist, Thinking Black* (Boston, MA: South End Press, 1989), 9.

8   DeLamotte, "Vision and Transformation," in *Women Imagine Change*, 401.

9   Chun, "Unbearable Witness," 114.

10 Ibid., 118. Some women at Ecole Polytechnique, for instance, rejected linking the Montreal massacre with violence against women and also rejected being described as feminists and/or victims. One woman insisted that feminist talk about women's struggles had nothing to do with her; women in their twenties did not have the same challenges and wounds as women in the generation preceding them. They were on a new road that older feminist could not understand (Chun 126–27).

11 Ibid., 138, 140.

12 Marian Yeo, "Murdered by Misogyny: Lin Gibson's Response to the Montreal Massacre," *Canadian Woman Studies* 12, no. 1 (Fall 1991): 8.

13 Ibid., 11.

14 Chris McDowell, interview by author, tape recording, Toronto, ON, June 15, 2003.

15 McDowell, interview, June 15, 2003.

16 Beth Abler, interview by author, tape recording, Toronto, ON, May 16, 2003.

17 "Marker of Change: The Story of the Women's Monument." http://www.movingimages.bc.ca/catalogue/Individual/Individual_m.html (accessed July 8, 2004).

18 Tourisme Montréal—Story Ideas. http://www.tourisme-montreal.org/Media_Target/HotTopics/EN/HTML/425_EN.asp (accessed July 12, 2004).

19 Rose Marie Goulet, interview by author, tape recording, Montreal, June 3, 2003.

20 Ailbhe Smyth, "Seeing Red: Men's Violence against Women in Ireland," in *Women in a Violent World: Feminist Analyses and Resistance across 'Europe,'* ed. Chris Corrin (Edinburgh University Press, 1996), 55.

21 Don't Remain Silent, Toronto: *A Space*, March 1991. The curator of the exhibit was Susan Beamish.

22 Kelly Aitken, "Fifteen Women," in Don't Remain Silent.

23 Gloria Escomel, "The Vicious Circle of Violence," in *The Montreal Massacre*, ed. Louise Malette and Marie Chalouh, trans. Marlene Wildeman (Charlottetown: gynergy books, 1991), 131.

24 Brian Wong, "Memories of Liberty and Fear," *Gazette*, November 15, 2002.

25 Sandra Coulson, "Bernice Vincent Reflection of Death: London Artist Explores 'The Moment You Draw in Your Breath.'" *London Free Press*, February 14, 1999, D1.

26 Wong, "Memories of Liberty and Fear," 7–8.

27 Bernice Vincent, interview by author, tape recording, London, May 24, 2003.

28 Maggie Helwig, interview by author, tape recording, Toronto, May 15, 2003.

29 Rita Beiks, interview by author, tape recording, Vancouver, June 18, 2003.

30 Martin Dufresne, interview by author, tape recording, Montreal, June 3, 2003.

31 Andrea Dworkin, "Terror, Torture and Resistance," *Canadian Woman Studies* 12, no. 1 (Fall 1991): 38–39.

32 Deirdre Hanna, "Healing Images Remembers Killings in Montreal," *Now*, November 8–14, 1990, 56.

33 Jane Davenport, "Feminist Label Won't Stick," *Gazette*, December 5, 1999, A8.

34 Monique Frize, interview by author, tape recording, Ottawa, June 4, 2003.
35 Michele Landsberg, interview by author, tape recording, Toronto, May 16, 2003.
36 Ibid.
37 Carol Shields, *The Stone Diaries* (Toronto: Vintage Books, 1993), 297.
38 Hildegard Westerkamp, interview by author, tape recording, Vancouver, June 19, 2003.
39 Ibid.
40 Tamara Bernstein, "Lament for the Women—Hildegard Westerkamp: Ecole Polytechnique," *Herizons* 7, no. 1 (January 3, 1993): 21.
41 Sharon Rosenberg, "Reflections on Memorializing December 6," *Resources for Feminist Research* 26, nos. 3–4 (Fall/Winter 1998/99): 204.
42 Sharon Rosenberg, "Inside the Ellipses: Intervals (of) (for) Memory," *Borderlines* 24, no. 5 (1992): 3.
43 Regina Coupar, interview by author, tape recording, Halifax, May 28, 2003.
44 Press conference, Downtown Eastside Women's Centre. http://www.dewc.ca (accessed June 26, 2002).
45 Pamela Harrison, interview by author, tape recording, Ottawa, May 28, 2003.
46 Landsberg, *Toronto Star*, December 5, 1999, A2.
47 Peter Davison, interview by author, tape recording, Halifax, May 30, 2003.
48 Michele Landsberg, "White Ribbon Tinged with Unease," *Toronto Star*, November 28, 1999: A2.
49 Harrison, interview, May 28, 2003.
50 Monique Frize, interview by author, tape recording, Ottawa, June 4, 2003.
51 Lynda Hurst, "The Massacre's Remarkable Legacy," *Toronto Star*, November 27, 1999, A4.
52 Ursula King, quoted in *Re-Visioning Our Sources: Women's Spirituality in European Perspectives*, ed. Annette Esser, Anne Overzee, and Susan Roll (Kampen: Kok Pharos, 1997), 129.
53 Maggie Helwig, "Flashpoint," *Matriart* 1, no. 1 (Spring 1990): 12.
54 Delamotte et al., Introduction, *Women Imagine Change*, 5.
55 Elaine Carol, interview by author, tape recording, Vancouver, June 17, 2003.
56 Delamotte, "Sexuality, Spirituality and Power," in *Women Imagine Change*, 15.
57 Carol Ann Weaver, interview by author, tape recording, Waterloo, ON, May 21, 2003.
58 See Cynthia Eller, "Feminist Politics and Feminist Spirituality," in Eller, *Living in the Lap of the Goddess* (New York: Crossroad, 1993), 185–207.
59 Dufresne, interview, Montreal, June 3, 2003.
60 Lois Wilson, "Rockers of the Cradle, Rockers of the Boat: Feminist Utopias," in *Feminist Utopias: Re-visioning Our Futures*, ed. Margrit Eichler, June Larkin, and Sheila Neysmith (Toronto: Inanna Publications and Education, 2002), 77.
61 Beiks, interview, Vancouver, June 18, 2003
62 Melanie Kaye/Kantrowitz, *The Issue Is Power: Essays on Women, Jews, Violence and Resistance* (San Francisco: Aunt Lute Books, 1992), 50.
63 Gregory Baum, *Essays in Critical Theology* (Kansas City: Sheed and Ward, 1994), 191.
64 Caputi and Russell, "'Femicide': Speaking the Unspeakable," 37.
65 Weaver, interview, Waterloo, ON, May 21, 2003.
66 Bernstein, "Lament for the Women," 21.

Conclusion

1 Northrop Frye, *The Bush Garden: Essays on the Canadian Imagination* (Toronto: Anansi Press, 1971), 220.

2 Christina Benson, "The War on Women," *Policy Options* 11, no. 10 (December 1990): 7–8.

3 Sherill Grace, *Violent Duality: A Study of Margaret Atwood* (Montreal: Véhicule Press, 1980), 42.

4 Margaret Atwood, "A Bus Along St. Clair: December," in Atwood, *Selected Poems* (Toronto: Oxford University Press, 1976), 116.

5 Beverly Wildung Harrison, "Theological Reflection in the Struggle for Liberation," in Harrison, *Making the Connections: Essays in Feminist Social Ethics*, ed. Carol S. Robb (Boston: Beacon Press, 1985), 261.

6 Nancy Hartsock, "Feminist Theory and Revolutionary Strategy," in *Capitalist Patriarchy and the Case for Feminist Socialism*, ed. Zillah Eisenstin (New York: Monthly Review Press, 1979), 64.

7 Sharon Welch, *Communities of Resistance and Solidarity: A Feminist Theology of Liberation* (Maryknoll, NY: Orbis Books, 1985), 56–57.

8 Ibid., 65.

9 Ibid., 71.

10 Michel Foucault, *Power/Knowledge: Selected Interviews and Other Writings, 1972–1977*, (New York: Random House, 1980), quoted in Welch, *Communities of Resistance*, 59.

11 Anthony Giddins, *Sociology: A Brief but Critical Introduction* (Toronto: Harcourt Brace Jovanovich, 1987), 12–13.

12 I owe this insight to Chris McDowell, Interview.

13 Perkei Avot, Ethics of Our Fathers, 2, no. 21. http://www.shechem.org/torah/avot.html (accessed August 18, 2003).

14 Alice Munro, *Something I've Been Meaning to Tell You* (Toronto: McGraw-Hill Ryerson, 1974), quoted in Eric Savoy, "The Antecedents of 'It': A Poetics of Absence," in *Open Letter* 7, no. 9 (Winter 1991): 96.

15 Dorothy E. Smith, "Institutional Ethnography: A Feminist Method," in *Gender and Society: Creating a Canadian Women's Sociology*, ed. Arlene Tigar McLaren (Toronto: Copp Clark Pitman, 1988), 77.

16 Gwendolyn MacEwen, "The Discovery," in *Poetry by Canadian Women*, ed. Rosemary Sullivan (Toronto: Oxford University Press, 1989), 163. Permission for use granted by the Author's family.

Appendix

1 Deena Metzger, *Writing for Your Life* (San Francisco: HarperSanFrancisco, 1992), 190.

2 Margaret Atwood, "Spelling," in Atwood, *True Stories* (Toronto: Oxford University Press, 1981), 64.

3 Stevie Cameron, "Our Daughters, Ourselves," *Globe and Mail* (Toronto), December 9, 1989, D1, D8.

4 Maria Harris, *Dance of the Spirit: The Seven Stages of Women's Spirituality* (New York: Bantam, 1991), 171.

Selected Bibliography

Adamson, Nancy, Linda Briskin, and Margaret McPhail. *Feminists Organizing for Change: The Contemporary Women's Movement in Canada.* Toronto: Oxford University Press, 1988.

Aptheker, Bettina. *Tapestries of Life: Women's Work, Women's Consciousness and the Meaning of Daily Experience.* Amherst, MA: University of Massachusetts Press, 1989.

Atwood, Margaret. *The Journals of Susanna Moodie.* Toronto: Oxford University Press, 1970.

———. *Selected Poems.* Toronto: Oxford University Press, 1976.

———. *True Stories.* Toronto: Oxford University Press, 1981.

Baril, Joan. "At the Centre of the Backlash." *Canadian Forum* 786 (February 1990): 14–17.

Baum, Gregory. "Afterword." In *Faith That Transforms: Essays in Honor of Gregory Baum,* ed. Mary Jo Leddy and Mary Ann Hinsdale, 135–51. New York: Paulist Press, 1987.

———. *Compassion and Solidarity: The Church for Others.* Massey Lectures. Toronto: CBC Enterprises, 1987.

———. "The Contemporary Social Gospel." In *Proceedings of the 1978 Conference of the Institute for Christian Life in Canada,* 1–17. Toronto: Institute for Christian Life in Canada, 1978.

———. "The Creed That Liberates." *Horizons* 13, no. 1 (Spring 1986): 136–49.

———. *Essays in Critical Theology.* Kansas City: Sheed and Ward, 1994.

———. "Faith and Liberation: Development since Vatican II." In Gregory Baum, *Theology and Society,* 3–31. New York: Paulist Press, 1987.

———. "God's Word as Judgement and New Life." *Chelsea Journal* 3, no. 3 (May–June 1977): 149–52.

———. "Gutierrez and the Catholic Tradition." *The Ecumenist* 21, no. 6 (September–October 1983): 81–84.

————. "The Homosexual Condition and Political Responsibility." In *A Challenge to Love: Gay and Lesbian Catholics in the Church*, ed. Robert Nugent, 38–51. New York: Crossroad, 1984.

————. "The Impact of Sociology on Catholic Theology." In *Theology and Sociology: A Reader*, ed. Robin Gill, 130–44. New York: Paulist Press, 1987.

————. "Literary Praxis." *The Ecumenist* 25, no. 4 (May–June 1987): 58–60.

————. "Middle Class Religion in America." In *Christianity and the Bourgeoisie. Concilium* 125, ed. Johannes Baptist Metz, 15–23. New York: Seabury Press, 1979.

————. "Option for the Powerless." *The Ecumenist* 26, no. 1 (November–December 1987): 5–11.

————. "Personal Testimony to Sociology." *The Ecumenist* 8, no. 1 (November–December 1969): 1–4.

————. "Political Theology in Canada." *The Ecumenist* 15, no. 3 (March–April 1977): 33–46.

————. "The Power of the Poor: Theological and Sociological Perspectives." *CTSA Proceedings* 37 (1982): 165–69.

————. "The Presence of the Church in Society." *Catholic Mind* (December 1970): 35–41.

————. *Religion and Alienation: A Theological Reading of Sociology*. New York: Paulist Press, 1975.

————. "Remarks of a Theologian in Dialogue with Sociology." In *Theology and the Social Sciences*, ed. Michael Horace Barnes, 3–11. Maryknoll, NY: Orbis Books, 2001.

————. "A Response to Haight, Hutchinson, Simpson, and Rotstein." *Toronto Journal of Theology* 3, no. 2 (Fall 1987): 203–208.

————. "Sociology and Salvation: Do We Need a Catholic Sociology?" *Theological Studies* 50, no. 4 (1989): 718–44.

————. "Theological Methodology: The Magisterium." *The Ecumenist* 27, no. 5 (July–August 1989): 71–74.

————. *Theology and Society*. New York: Paulist Press, 1987.

————. "Theology in the Americas: Detroit II." *The Ecumenist* 18, no. 6 (September–October 1980): 90–94.

————. *Truth beyond Relativism: Karl Mannheim's Sociology of Knowledge*. Milwaukee: Marquette University Press, 1977.

Baum, Gregory, ed. *Journeys: The Impact of Personal Experience on Religious Thought*. New York: Paulist Press, 1975.

Benson, Christina. "The War on Women," *Policy Options* 11, no. 10 (December 1990): 7–12.

Bergman, Brian. "Sisterhood of Fear and Fury." *Maclean's*, December 18, 1989, 18–19.

Bernstein, Tamara. "Lament for the Women." *Herizons*, January 3, 1993, 20–23.

Bertrand, Marie-Andrée. "Analyse criminologique d'un meurtre commis dans l'enceinte de l'université et des interprétations que certains groupes choisissent d'en donner." *Sociologie et Sociétés* 22, no. 1 (April 1990): 193–97.

Brossard, Nicole, et al. "One Year After." *This Magazine*, December–January 1991, 16–23.

Canada. *Changing the Landscape: Ending Violence—Achieving Equality*. Final Report of the Canadian Panel on Violence against Women. Ottawa, 1993.

Canada. Standing Committee on Health and Welfare, Social Affairs, Seniors and the Status of Women. *The War against Women*. Ottawa: June 1991.

Caputi, Jane, and Diana Russell. "'Femicide': Speaking the Unspeakable." *Ms.* September–October 1990, 34–37.

Chun, Wendy Hui-Kyong. "Unbearable Witness: Toward a Politics of Listening." *Differences: A Journal of Feminist Cultural Studies* 11, no. 1 (1999): 112–49.

Code, Lorraine. "Credibility: A Double Standard." In *Feminist Perspectives: Philosophical Essays on Method and Morals*, ed. Lorraine Code, Sheila Mullett, and Christine Overall, 64–88. Toronto: University of Toronto Press, 1988.

Cook, Katherine Margaret. "Women's Sociology." M.A. thesis, Ontario Institute for Studies in Education, 1979.

Corrin, Chris, ed. *Women in a Violent World: Feminist Analyses and Resistance across "Europe."* Edinburgh: Edinburgh University Press, 1996.

Courville, Louis. "J'étais Là." *Women in Scholarship: One Step Forward, Two Steps Back? Royal Society of Canada Proceedings*, 1–2 (University of Victoria, June 3 1990).

Delamotte, Eugenia C., Natania Meeker, and Jean O'Barr, eds. *Women Imagine Change: A Global Anthology of Women's Resistance from 600 B.C.E. to Present*. New York: Routledge, 1997.

Dorscht, Susan Rudy. "Writing at the Interval." *Open Letter* 7, no. 9 (Winter 1991): 100–11.

Dworkin, Andrea. "Terror, Torture and Resistance." *Canadian Woman Studies* 12, no. 1 (Fall 1991): 37–42.

Elgin, Peter, and Stephen Hester. *The Montreal Massacre: A Story of Membership Categorization Analysis*. Waterloo, ON: Wilfrid Laurier University Press, 2003.

Eller, Cynthia. *Living in the Lap of the Goddess*. New York: Crossroad, 1993.

El Yamani, Myriame. "La mascarade médiatique." *Sociologie et Sociétés* 22, no. 1 (April 1990): 201–205.

Esser, Annette, Anne Overzee, and Susan Roll, eds. *Re-Visioning Our Sources: Women's Spirituality in European Perspectives*. Kampen: Kok Pharos, 1997.

Evans, Ruth. "'Behold I Am Doing a New Thing': Canadian Feminist Theology and the Social Gospel." In *A Long and Faithful March: "Towards the Christian Revolution," 1930's/1980's*, ed. Harold Wells and Roger Hutchinson, 153–65. Toronto: United Church Publishing House, 1989.

Franklin, Ursula. "Community and Technology." *Canadian Forum* 791 (July–August 1990): 20–23.

Freed, Josh. "Soul Searching in Montreal and Canada." *Canadian Dimension* 24, no. 2 (March 1990): 17.

Freire, Paulo. *Pedagogy of the Oppressed*. New York: Seabury Press, 1970.

Frize, Monique. "The Bold and the Brave: Women Engineers Striving for Change." CD-ROM Proceedings of the ICWES12 Conference, Ottawa, July 2002.

Frye, Northrop. *The Bush Garden: Essays on the Canadian Imagination*. Toronto: Anansi Press, 1971.

Gabor, Thomas. "The Federal Gun Registry: An Urgent Need for Independent, Non-partisan Research," *Canadian Journal of Criminology and Criminal Justice* 45, no. 4 (October 2003): 489–98.

Gartner, Rosemary, Myrna Dawson, and Maria Crawford. "Woman Killing: Intimate Femicide in Ontario, 1974–1994." *Resources for Feminist Research* 26, nos. 3–4 (Fall–Winter 1998/99): 151–73.

Giddins, Anthony. *Sociology: A Brief but Critical Introduction*. Toronto: Harcourt Brace Jovanovich, 1987.

Gill, Robin, ed. *Theology and Sociology: A Reader*. New York: Paulist Press, 1987.

Grace, Sherill. *Violent Duality: A Study of Margaret Atwood*. Montreal: Véhicule Press, 1980.

Greenhill, Pauline. "A Good Start: A Graffiti Interpretation of the Montreal Massacre." *Atlantis* 17, no. 2 (Spring–Summer 1992): 106–18.

Haight, Roger. Review of *Theology and Society*, by Gregory Baum. *Studies in Religion* 81, no. 1 (1989): 97–99.

Hanna, Deirdre. "Healing Images Remembers Killings in Montreal." *Now*, November 8–14 1990, 56.

Harding, Sandra, ed. *Feminism and Methodology: Social Science Issues*. Bloomington, IN: Indiana University Press, 1987.

Harris, Debbie Wise. "Keeping Women in Our Place." *Canadian Woman Studies* 11, no. 4 (Summer 1991): 37–41.

Harris, Maria. *Dance of the Spirit: The Seven Stages of Women's Spirituality*. New York: Bantam, 1991.

Harrison, Beverly Wildung. "Agendas for a New Theological Ethic." In *Churches in Struggle: Liberation Theologies and Social Change in North America*, ed. William Tabb, 89–98. New York: Monthly Review Press, 1986.

Harrison, Beverly Wildung. *Making the Connections: Essays in Feminist Social Ethics*. Ed. Carol S. Robb. Boston: Beacon Press, 1985.

Hartsock, Nancy. "Feminist Theory and the Development of Revolutionary Strategy." In *Capitalist Patriarchy and the Case for Socialist Feminism*, ed. Zillah Eisenstein, 56–77. New York: Monthly Review Press, 1979.

Haskell, Lori, and Melanie Randall. "The Politics of Women's Safety: Sexual Violence, Women's Fear and the Public/Private Split." *Resources for Feminist Research* 26, nos. 3–4 (Fall/Winter 1998/99): 113–49.

Helwig, Maggie. "Flashpoint," *Matriart* 1, no. 1 (Spring 1990): 12.

Heyward, Carter. "The Power of God-with-Us." *Christian Century* 107, no. 1 (March 14, 1990): 275–78.

hooks, bell. *Talking Back: Thinking Feminist, Thinking Black*. Boston, MA: South End Press, 1989.

Jelliffe, Vaughn. "How PEI Women's Groups Responded to the Murder of 14 Students in Montreal." *Common Ground* 9, no. 1 (February 1990): 8.

Kafer, Rudy, Barbara Hodkin, David Furrow and Trudy Lancry, "What Do the Montreal Murders Mean? Attitudinal and Demographic Predictors of Attribution." *Canadian Journal of Behavioural Science* 25, no. 4 (October 1993): 541–58.

Kaye/Kantrowitz, Melanie. *The Issue Is Power: Essays on Women, Jews, Violence and Resistance* San Francisco: Aunt Lute Books, 1992.

Kennedy, Rose Marie. "Remembering Montreal: For a Future without Fear." *Kinesis*, December–January 1992.

Lacroix, Margot. "Slowing Down the Process of Forgetting." Review of *The Montreal Massacre*, edited by Louise Malette and Marie Chalouh. *Kinesis*, October 1991, 14.

Lash, Nicholas. *A Matter of Hope*. Notre Dame, IN: University of Notre Dame Press, 1981.

Lakeman, Lee. "Women, Violence and the Montreal Massacre." *This Magazine*, March 1990, 20–23.

Lévesque, Marie-Claire. "The Panel on Violence against Women: Another Smoke Screen?" *Canadian Woman Studies* 12, no. 1 (Fall 1991): 117–18.

Luxton, Meg, and Sue Findlay. "Is the Everyday World the Problematic? Reflections on Smith's Method of Making Sense of Women's Experience." *Studies in Political Economy* 30 (Autumn 1989): 183–96.

Malette, Louise, and Marie Chalouh, eds. *The Montreal Massacre*. Translated by Marlene Wildeman. Charlottetown, PE: gynergy books, 1991.

McQuarrie, Fiona. "Letter to the Editor." *This Magazine*, August 1990, 10.

Metzger, Deena. *Writing for Your Life*. San Francisco: HarperSanFrancisco, 1992.

Mies, Marie. "Towards a Methodology for Feminist Research." In *Theories of Women's Studies*, ed. Gloria Bowles and Renata Duelli Klein, 122–27. New York: Routledge & Kegan Paul, 1983.

Miller, Leslie. Review of *The Everyday World as Problematic*, by Dorothy E. Smith. *Canadian Journal of Sociology* 14, no. 4 (Fall 1989): 521–31.

Mitchell, Penni. "What Has to Happen to Stop the Violence?" *Herizons*, Spring 1992, 16–29.

Moodie, Susanna. *Roughing It in the Bush*. Toronto: McClelland and Stewart, 1923.

Morgan, Patricia. "From Battered Wife to Program Client: The State's Shaping of Social Problems." *Kapitalistate* 9 (1981): 17–39.

Morris, Marika. "Factsheet: Violence against Women and Girls." Canadian Research Institute for the Advancement of Women, 2002.

Murray, Heather. "Women in the Wilderness." In *A Mazing Space: Writing Canadian Women Writing*, ed. Shirley Neuman and Smaro Kamboureli, 74–83. Edmonton: Longspoon/NeWest, 1986.

Nelson-McDermott, Catherine. "Murderous Fallout: Post-Lépine Rhethoric." *Atlantis* 17, no. 1 (Fall–Winter 1991): 124–28.

Radical Lesbian Group. "Insignificant Violence?" *Connexions* 34 (1990): 8–10.

Rathjen, Heidi, and Charles Montpetit. *December 6: From the Montreal Massacre to Gun Control: The Inside Story*. Toronto: McClelland and Stewart, 1999.

Roach Pierson, Ruth. "Violence against Women: Strategies for Change." *Canadian Woman Studies* 11, no. 4 (Summer 1991): 10–12.

Rosenberg, Jerome. *Margaret Atwood*. Boston: Twayne Publishers, 1984.

Rosenberg, Sharon. "Inside the Ellipses: Intervals (of) (for) Memory." *Borderlines* 24, no. 5 (1992): 30–35.

———. "Reflections on Memorializing December 6." *Resources for Feminist Research* 26, nos. 3–4 (Fall–Winter 1998/99): 203–12.

Ruether, Rosemary Radford. *Sexism and God-Talk: Toward a Feminist Theology*. Boston: Beacon Press, 1983.

Savoy, Eric. "The Antecedents of 'It': A Poetics of Absence." *Open Letter* 7, no. 9 (Winter 1991): 88–99.

Schild, Veronica. "The Eclipse of Criticalness in Marxist Social Science: Habermas and Smith." M.A. thesis, Ontario Institute for Studies in Education, 1982.

Schmidt, Lisa. "Sorrow, Anger after Montreal." *Kinesis*, February 1990, 7.

Schüssler Fiorenza, Elisabeth. *In Memory of Her: A Feminist Theological Reconstruction of Christian Origins*. New York: Crossroads, 1983.

Shapiro, Ivor. "Why Did Marc Lépine Murder 14 Women?" *Chatelaine*, June 1990, 41–43, 74–76.

Sheinin, Rose. "La Suite du 6 Décembre." *Women in Scholarship: One Step Forward, Two Steps Back? Royal Society of Canada Proceedings* (University of Victoria, June 3, 1990): 3–9.

Shields, Carol. *The Stone Diaries*. Toronto: Vintage Press, 1993.

Simpson, John. "Gregory Baum and Sociology." *Toronto Journal of Theology* 3, no. 2 (Fall 1987): 194–98.

Smith, Dorothy E. "An Analysis of Ideological Structures and How Women Are Excluded: Considerations for Academic Women." *Canadian Review of Sociology and Anthropology* 12, no. 4 (1975): 353–70.

———. *The Conceptual Practices of Power: A Feminist Sociology of Knowledge*. Boston: Northeastern University Press, 1990.

———. "The Deep Structure of Gender Antithesis: Another View of Capitalism and Patriarchy." In *Feminist Ethic for Social Science Research*, Nebraska Sociological Feminist Collective, 23–35. Leviston, NY: Edwin Mellen Press, 1988.

———. "Editor's Introduction: On Sally L. Hacker's Method." In *Doing It the Hard Way: Investigations of Gender and Technology*, ed. Dorothy E. Smith and Susan M. Turner, 1–17. Boston: Unwin Hyman, 1990.

———. *The Everyday World as Problematic.* Toronto: University of Toronto Press, 1987.

———. "Feminism and the Malepractice of Sociology." *Popular Feminism Papers* 3. Toronto: Ontario Institute for Studies in Education (OISE), 1986.

———. *Feminism and Marxism: A Place to Begin and a Way to Go.* Vancouver: New Star Books, 1977.

———. "Feminist Reflections on Political Economy." *Studies in Political Economy* 30 (Autumn 1989): 37–59.

———. "Gender, Power and Peace." In *Up and Doing: Canadian Women and Peace*, ed. Janice Williamson and Deborah Gorham, 93–100. Toronto: Women's Press, 1989.

———. "The Ideological Practice of Sociology." *Catalyst* 8 (1974): 39–54.

———. "Institutional Ethnography: A Feminist Method." In *Gender and Society: Creating a Canadian Women's Sociology*, ed. Arlene Tigar McLaren, 62–79. Toronto: Copp Clark Pitman, 1988.

———. "K Is Mentally Ill: The Anatomy of a Factual Account." *Sociology* 12, no. 1 (1978): 23–53.

———. "On Sociological Description: A Method from Marx." *Human Studies* 4 (1981): 313–37.

———. "Some Implications of a Sociology for Women." In *Women in a Man-Made World: A Socio-Economic Handbook*, ed. Nona Glazer and Helen Waehrer, 15–29. Chicago: Rand-McNally, 1977.

———. "Sociological Theory: Methods of Writing Patriarchy." In *Feminism and Sociological Theory*, ed. Ruth A. Wallace, 34–64. Newbury Park, CA: Sage, 1989.

———. "A Sociology for Women." In *The Prism of Sex: Essays in the Sociology of Knowledge*, ed. J. Sherman and F. Beck, 135–87. Madison, WI: University of Wisconsin Press, 1979.

———. "The Statistics on Mental Illness: What They Will Not Tell Us about Women and Why." In *Women Look at Psychiatry*, ed. Dorothy E. Smith and Sarah Davids, 73–119. Vancouver: Press Gang, 1975.

———. *Texts, Facts, and Femininity: Exploring the Relations of Ruling.* New York: Routledge, 1990.

———. "Textually Mediated Social Organization." *International Social Science Journal* 36, no. 1 (1984): 59–75.

———. "What It Might Mean to Do a Canadian Sociology: The Everyday World as Problematic." *Canadian Journal of Sociology* 1, no. 3 (Fall 1975): 363–76.

———. "Where There Is Oppression There Is Resistance." *Branching Out* 6, no. 1 (1979): 10–15.

———. "Women's Perspective as a Radical Critique of Sociology." In *Feminism and Methodology: Social Science Issues*, ed. Sandra Harding, 84–96. Bloomington, IN: Indiana University Press, 1987.

Smith, Dorothy E., and Varda Burstyn. *Women, Class, Family and the State*. Toronto: Garamond Press, 1985.

Smith, Dorothy E., and Alison Griffith. "Constructing Cultural Knowledge: Mothering as Discourse." In *Women and Education: A Canadian Perspective*, ed. Jane Gaskell and Arlene McLaren, 87–104. Calgary, AB: Detselig Enterprises, 1987.

Smith, Dorothy E., and Naomi Hersom, "Women and the Canadian Labour Force." Ottawa: Social Sciences and Humanities Research Council of Canada, 1982.

Smith, Dorothy E., and Sarah Davids, eds. *Women Look at Psychiatry*. Vancouver: Press Gang, 1975.

Storrie, Kathleen. "The Everyday World as Problematic: A Bridge between the Academy and the University." In *From the Margins to the Centre: Essays in Women's Studies Research*, ed. Dawn Currie, 122–33. Saskatoon, SK: Women's Studies Research Unit, 1988.

Sullivan, Rosemary, ed. *Poetry by Canadian Women*. Toronto: Oxford University Press, 1989.

Tyler, Ann. "Still Just Writing." In *The Writer on Her Work: Contemporary Women Writers Reflect on Their Art and Situation*, ed. Janet Steinberg, 3–16. New York: W.W. Norton, 1980.

Walker, Gillian. *Family Violence and the Women's Movement*. Toronto: University of Toronto Press, 1990.

Wallace, Bronwen. *Common Magic*. Toronto: Oberon Press, 1985.

———. *The Stubborn Particulars of Grace*. Toronto: McClelland & Stewart, 1987.

Wallace, Bruce. "The Making of a Mass Killer." *Maclean's*, December 18, 1989, 22.

Welch, Sharon. *Communities of Resistance and Solidarity: A Feminist Theology of Liberation*. Maryknoll, NY: Orbis Books, 1985.

Westkott, Marcia. "Feminist Criticism of the Social Sciences." *Harvard Educational Review* 49 (November 1979): 422–30.

Williamson, Janice. "'The Landscape from How I See My Poems Moving': An Interview with Bronwen Wallace." *Open Letter* 7, no. 9 (Winter 1991): 26–35.

Wilson, Lois. "Rockers of the Cradle, Rockers of the Boat: Feminist Utopias." In *Feminist Utopias: Re-visioning Our Futures*, ed. Margrit Eichler, June Larkin, and Sheila Neysmith. Toronto: Inanna Publications and Education, 2002.

Yeo, Marian. "Murdered by Misogyny: Lin Gibson's Response to the Montreal Massacre." *Canadian Woman Studies* 12, no. 1 (Fall 1991): 8–11.

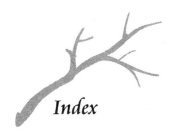

Index

Series Published by Wilfrid Laurier University Press for the Canadian Corporation for Studies in Religion/ Corporation Canadienne des Sciences Religieuses

Series numbers not mentioned are out of print.

Editions SR

The Study of Religion in Canada /
Sciences Religieuses au Canada

Studies in Women and Religion /
Études sur les femmes et la religion

*Available only from Les Presses de l'Université Laval

SR Supplements

Series discontinued

Available from:
Wilfrid Laurier University Press
Waterloo, Ontario, Canada N2L 3C5
Telephone: (519) 884-0710, ext. 6124
Fax: (519) 725-1399
E-mail: press@wlu.ca
Website: http://www.wlupress.wlu.ca